# TRANSRACIAL

# COMMUNICATION

**Arthur L. Smith**

*University of California, Los Angeles*

PRENTICE-HALL, INC.
Englewood Cliffs, New Jersey

*Library of Congress Cataloging in Publication Data*

SMITH, Arthur Lee,
  Transracial communication.

  (Prentice-Hall speech communication series)
  Bibliography: p.
  1. Intercultural communication. 2. Speech and social status. 3. Negroes—Language. 4. Social conflict. I. Title.
HM258.S537    301.14    72–10169
ISBN 0–13–929505–4
ISBN 0–13–929497–X (pbk)

**PRENTICE-HALL SPEECH COMMUNICATION SERIES**

Larry L. Barker and Robert J. Kibler,
*Consulting Editors*

© 1973 by PRENTICE-HALL, INC.
*Englewood Cliffs, New Jersey*

10  9  8  7  6  5  4  3  2  1

Printed in the United States of America

Prentice-Hall International, Inc., *London*
Prentice-Hall of Australia, Pty., Inc., *Sydney*
Prentice-Hall of Canada, Ltd., *Toronto*
Prentice-Hall of India Private Limited, *New Delhi*
Prentice-Hall of Japan, Inc., *Tokyo*

# Contents

PREFACE                                                    v

**one**
INTRODUCTION                                               1

**two**
DIRECTIONS IN
TRANSRACIAL COMMUNICATION                                  7

    Definitions   9; Process   11; Structurization   12;
    Purpose   14.

**three**
CULTURE AND
TRANSRACIAL COMMUNICATION                                  23

    A Viewpoint on Culture   25; Time   30; Family   35;
    Black Language Styles   36; Functions of Black Language   41;
    An Approach to Intervention   43.

**four**
STRUCTURE OF
TRANSRACIAL COMMUNICATION                                  47

    Form and Content   49; Qualities Affecting Structure   51.

Contents

**five**
*A MODEL OF
TRANSRACIAL COMMUNICATION*                                          *61*

Universal Context   65; Ethnic Perspective   66;
Initiator   67.

**six**
*ELEMENTS OF
TRANSRACIAL NOISE*                                                  *69*

Control Beliefs   71; Stereotypes   74;
Lack of Basic Skills   75; Inadequate Perception   76.

**seven**
*SYMBOLS IN
TRANSRACIAL COMMUNICATION*                                          *81*

Symbols   84; Symbols and Racism   91.

**eight**
*DETERMINANTS
OF NORMALIZATION*                                                   *99*

Speech Acts in Transracial Contexts   101;
Metacommunication   103;
Sex and Transracial Communication   105;
Social Stratification and Transracial Interaction   111;
Conversations in the Routine   129;
Consensus:   The Plague of Normalization   133.

*BIBLIOGRAPHY*                                                      *137*

*INDEX*                                                             *149*

# Preface

This manuscript is the product of an intellectual adventure supported in part by an earnest eclecticism. It is a book about how human beings, in the course of interacting, come to communicate effectively with those of different ethnic or racial groups. While it deals with human behavior and bases many of its concepts upon behavioral research, it also contains systematic subjective discussions of how communication is patterned in transracial situations.

Communicating with another person is a multifaceted event involving psychological, physiological, and physical processes. How persons send and receive messages from other persons who do not share similar histories, heritages, or cultures is of critical importance to our understanding of contemporary society.

Working with Professor Jere Veilleux of Purdue University and later with Professor Andrea Rich of the University of California, Los Angeles, to establish courses in Interracial Communication, I became annoyed that no text could be found that would adequately represent concepts that needed to be discussed.

Because conventional works of communication

theory seldom treat transracial constructs, this book draws heavily upon several fields in an effort to synthesize factual information for a concise presentation of transracial communication concepts. For this reason, much that is written in this volume is of a heuristic character. Its purpose is to define an area, raise questions, and advance answers. Therefore, this text is not an encyclopedia of communication theory; rather, it is an approach to transracial communication. And in a kind of introductory way, it has endeavored to provide ideas that will educe discussion.

Communication is, in the most elemental sense, sharing. When persons of different ethnic backgrounds communicate, they grant and receive the privilege of participating with each other. The more perfect the understanding of the message, the more complete the communication. This being the case, it is almost miraculous that persons of the same ethnic or cultural background communicate, not to speak of transracial communicators. But speak of them through these pages, we did.

I am indebted to a number of persons for their assistance and advice in the preparation of this book. Sociologist James Pitts has staunchly defended quite different views on cultural factors in communication and has kept me keen on the criticisms I am sure to receive. Communication theorists Larry Barker and Robert Kibler have isolated theoretical and technical matters that needed tending to and have provided me with every assistance. In the end, however, the judgments and conclusions have been mine, and I am wholly responsible for them. Among my students, Melbourne Cummings, Karen Borden, Jack Neiman, and Lynda Toth have been constant debaters and discussants. They have helped to refine and clarify my concepts, and many of their suggestions have probably been assimilated without specific acknowledgement. Finally, I am thankful to the UCLA Center for Afro-American Studies and the UCLA Academic Senate for grants that allowed me to complete this manuscript. The section on symbols was done with the assistance of a Ford Foundation grant administered by the UCLA Institute of American Cultures.

**Arthur L. Smith,**
*Visiting Professor,*
*Tallahassee, Florida*

# one

# *INTRODUCTION*

# Objectives

AFTER READING THE INTRODUCTION, YOU SHOULD
BE ABLE TO:

1. *Explain the rationale behind this book.*
2. *Describe what this work seeks to accomplish.*
3. *Discuss the possibility of race as a variable in communication.*
4. *Discuss whether you agree or disagree that the situation in the small integrated tool company was due to race, class, or merely individual differences.*

It is a truism that men become more interested in an area of study precisely when the normal patterns and styles of behavior seem to depend upon an understanding of that area. We seek to grasp those principal concepts, paradigms, and ideas that challenge our thinking or impinge upon our daily existence with such force that we are provoked to action. Unquestionably, men are more inclined to explore those fields of knowledge relating closely to their survival. Since our society and other multiethnic societies are likely to be involved in improving intercultural communication intranationally, we might profitably examine the processes and possibilities of transracial communication.

This book attempts to explore and explain communication among different racial groups within the scope of existing communication theory. This approach allows us to discuss the subject in terms that are familiar to students and scholars of human communication. What is unique, however, is the emphasis on communication within transracial contexts. Such a study seeks to add to our knowledge of interpersonal communication by examining the constraints and pressures present in transracial verbal interaction.

Readers may, of course, question whether these constraints and pressures are not applicable much more generally to all forms of human communication. Some might argue that the present book repeats communication principles discussed in other studies. Any resolution of these problems must consider the broad scope of communication theory to see how this book raises significant questions and makes peculiar application of those fundamental principles to transracial contexts. Thus, although the components of the communication process remain the same, the strictures upon that process might differ in transracial as opposed into intraracial situations. What we are attempting here is a concentrated effort to explore the process of communication as it occurs not between people of the same race but between different racial groups. In such an effort, the whole question of race as a variable in effective verbal interaction is raised once more. As the reader, you might want to reflect on your own attempts to communicate with someone of another race. Occasionally we do well; at other times there seems to be a barrier between us and the other fellow. Although this condition may and does arise in intraracial communication, it is never so sharp as in interracial contexts.

Since little has been done in this area before now, it would be presumptuous indeed to claim that this small book is definitive. Nor can it be claimed that we have identified through a heuristic development every possible direction for this area of study. Transracial communication is an exciting field, if for no other reason than that it offers hope for human problems. But this is not to suggest that we have provided the single panacea for difficulties that have troubled societies for years on end. We have not presented *the* solution. We have only begun to see clearly what the basic problems are, but that sight has led us to make some careful notations about interpersonal communication within transracial contexts. The reader will find in this book an account of some characteristics of transracial communication that the author has found worthy of consideration in seeking to understand its constraints and pressures.

Actually, transracial difficulties have seldom been explored in terms of fundamental communication problems that might be avoided by effectively manipulating symbols and signs. Too often, when persons of different ethnic backgrounds have problems relating to each other, they resort to "attack" words and name-calling, aiming at the other person's character, intelligence, or integrity. The disgruntled person blames the difficulty in communication on the other's dishonesty or stupidity. In a number of cases involving blacks and whites, this can be seen with unusual clarity.

Although blacks and whites living in America have many common experiences, values, and aspirations, there are numerous instances where communication lags because of misunderstandings. Here is one example.

In a small integrated tool company, the co-owners, one white and one black, had been trying to increase the efficiency of their company. Observing that one of the workers had been slacking off for several days, the owners warned him that if he did not start concentrating on his work, he would be fired. One day the white co-owner found the worker sleeping on the job. He summarily dismissed him. The worker appealed to the black co-owner, telling him that he was behind in his home mortgage and had taken on an extra job to avoid foreclosure, and that if he lost his job at the tool company, he would lose his home and not be able to support his wife and six children. The owners discussed the situation, the white owner arguing that they needed to maintain efficient operations and the black one sympathizing with the worker's problems. They finally decided to loan him the money at low interest so that he could quit his extra job and maintain his position with the company.

The example above is by no means categorical, but as we shall see, these types of problems arise between blacks and whites in American society more often than we like to admit. Some will argue vigorously that the basis for this kind of difficulty is cultural, but as Edward Hall contends, culture involves communication.[1] More directly, the question of the "subcultural" and "culturally deprived" within American society will be dealt with in a later chapter.

No book is written without the conscious or unconscious influence of others, and certainly these pages reflect my debt. Those from whom I have gained invaluable insight might also find some useful concepts and revelations in this book. The social psychologist, sociologist, anthropologist, and linguistician should find some ideas with pedagogical applicability. My colleagues in the field of speech communication should sense the potentialities inherent within communication paradigms for a multiethnic society.

[1] Edward T. Hall, *The Silent Language* (New York: Fawcett Books, 1959), p. 13.

# two

# *DIRECTIONS IN TRANSRACIAL COMMUNICATION*

# Objectives

AFTER READING THIS CHAPTER, YOU SHOULD BE ABLE TO:

1. *Define* transracial communication *and* ethnic group.
2. *Describe in writing how the process of communication involves initiators, messages, and media.*
3. *Explain how the author uses* structurization.
4. *Demonstrate in writing how the models proposed by Barnlund and Dance operate.*

# DEFINITIONS

## Transracial

$A$ll analyses end in definition; this book is no different. When you have completed reading the last page of this book, you will have experienced my definition of the subject. In this sense, the definitional context of a topic, subject, or term might conceivably include the total treatise being written about the term as topic. Additionally, it is possible to enlarge the context to include all experiences and observations of the author, and then to call that the definitional context of a term. One might go even further and include the influences upon the writer, the society, the world, and the universe. Generally, however, when a definition is sought for a term, we seek a more limited context. Thus, with some distillation of the macrocosmic picture, we can usually hazard a relatively short and sweet definition.

*Transracial* means *crossing racial lines*. To be sure, anthropologists are still not certain what is meant by *race*, so an additional, although not synonymous term, *interethnic*, can be used to zero in on our area of concern. Broadly speaking, a race may include several ethnic groupings. Therefore, *interethnic* is not the same as *transracial*, but it gives an additional dimension to our focus.

An *ethnic group* is one that *has shared a common heritage, history, culture; has experienced similar frustra-*

9

*tions and anxieties; and aspires to similar goals and aims.*
Biologically speaking, a person may be 80 percent one
race and yet identify with an ethnic group not usually
associated with his biological race. Ethnic identity, then,
can be determined by both birth and choice. Although
this book uses the general title *Transracial Communication*, it is concerned as much with interethnic communication.

## Communication

What it is precisely that can be called "communication" has exercised the minds of numerous scholars.[1] The
definition used in this book borrows from previous conceptualizations. We shall take the word *communication*
to mean *the symbolic interaction by which humans relate to each other.* The symbols—verbal, gestural, or pictorial—act as stimuli to evoke behavior in another person. In addition, communication may include what Sapir
called the "unconscious assimilation of the ideas and behavior of one's culture."[2] Thus, with the awareness of
cultural influences, an added dimension is provided for
our discussion of *transracial communication.* For what

[1]George A. Lundberg, *Foundations of Sociology* (New York: The
Macmillan Company, 1939), p. 253; Edward Sapir, "Communication,"
in *Encyclopedia of the Social Sciences* (New York: The Macmillan
Company, 1933), Vol. IV, p. 79; Theodore Newcomb, *Personality and
Social Change* (New York: Holt, Rinehart & Winston, Inc., 1957), pp.
288–90; Leonard W. Doob, *Communication in Africa* (New Haven:
Yale University Press, 1961), pp. 8–10; George A. Miller, *Language
and Communication* (New York: McGraw-Hill Book Company, 1951),
pp. 1–9; and Larry L. Barker and Robert J. Kibler, "A Conceptual Over-
view of Communication Dimensions," in Larry L. Barker and Robert
J. Kibler (eds.), *Speech Communication Behavior* (Englewood Cliffs,
N.J.: Prentice-Hall, Inc., 1971), pp. 2–10.
[2]Sapir, "Communication," *passim.*

**10**

our cultural context has made of us is what we convey to others. When someone acquires an impression of another, something is being communicated. The question of intention—that is, whether communication is classified as "explicit" or "implicit," as "indirect" or "direct"— must be viewed in the light of *humans relating to each other*. In other words, there are instances when we are influenced by stimuli not meant to influence us. And yet, because we are uniquely equipped to respond to certain kinds of stimuli, there is a natural reaction to those stimuli when they occur near us. We relate as human beings to other human beings through symbolic interaction whether the stimulus is intended or unintended. So while our analysis of transracial communication is primarily concerned with the conscious efforts of communicators, unconscious stimuli and responses often come into our purview.

## PROCESS

The process of communication involves initiators, messages, and media in dynamic interaction. Initiators may be categorized as primary and secondary. The primary initiator corresponds to the source and encoder in models; the secondary initiator corresponds to the receiver and decoder in the same models. The term *initiator* suggests that all participants in communication provoke reaction and response, even if the reaction is simply to ignore the other person. Dynamic interaction is more than linkage between two or more persons in communication; it refers to linkage in a certain way. *Linkage* can be a neutral term, but dynamic interaction suggests *re-*

*curring linkages.* In other words, to interact is more than mere connection, as *linkage* might suggest to some; it is the constant process of securing connection between communicators. In saying "process of securing connection," we deal with the fact that interaction is not static or lineal but involves periods of linkage and periods of nonlinkage. It is recurring linkage, and as such, dynamic interaction is the process of securing connection; in fact, it is a continuous attempt to establish linkage. So to speak of interaction simply as linkage is to misrepresent the communicative event.

Confrontation between human beings is by nature dynamic. Of course, the degree of involvement, action, and drama depends in large part upon predispositional initiators and situational contingencies. But because people are dynamic when in the company of other people, it is easy for us to understand how all participants in a communicative event can be called initiators. And the role of primary or secondary initiator alternates between participants.

## STRUCTURIZATION

The structured content produced by an initiator is called the *message.* Consisting of symbols and signs that must be mutually understandable by all communicators, the message provides the meaning for the dynamic interaction. Fearing has observed that the structure of the stimulus field may be either simple or complex, and in the spatial or temporal dimensions or both.[3] Messages come in many forms, however; verbal messages in inter-

[3]Franklin Fearing, "Toward a Psychological Theory of Human Communication," *Journal of Psychology,* 22 (1953), 73.

personal communication within transracial contexts tend to be structurally simple interchanges. This is not to say that the messages are never complex; indeed, they are, and because of this complexity, interracial communication can often be even more difficult than usual.

Two communication models developed in recent years have particular pertinence to transracial interaction.[4] Barnlund proposed a transactional model that postulates, among other things, that communication is dynamic and continuous.[5] In this sense, it exists as a continuing condition of life that fluctuates with our needs and desires. The ceaseless seeking and occasional finding of transracial communication attests to the continuous nature of the process on both the interpersonal and societal levels. Dance developed a helical model that purports to demonstrate how communication moves upward and inward simultaneously, allowing the initiator to be affected by his own past conformations as charted by the helix.[6] The structurizations of transracial communication may be thought of as affecting the future behavior of the communicators, inasmuch as we tend to monitor and are inclined, where possible, to minimize contradictions. Barnlund allows us to see the inner dynamics of communication, while Dance's helix serves to demonstrate that the communication process is continually moving forward; yet it is always to some degree dependent upon the past, which influences the present and the future.

Both models have relevance to transracial communi-

[4]See Dean C. Barnlund, "A Transactional Model of Communication," pp. 83–102, and Frank E. X. Dance, "A Helical Model of Communication," pp. 103–7, in Kenneth K. Sereno and C. David Mortensen (eds.), *Foundations of Communication Theory* (New York: Harper and Row, Publishers, 1970).
[5]Barnlund, "Transactional Model," in Sereno and Mortensen.
[6]Dance, "Helical Model," in Sereno and Mortensen.

cation as transaction or process but, like other communication models, fail to consider the relevancy of the special concerns of an interethnic or transracial dimension of the process.[7] My assumption is not that these models are not correct, or that they do not work, but that they are incomplete and tell us nothing about the constraints of interpersonal communication across racial lines. It is as if the model makers had conceived of all situations as being homogeneous. The structural integrity of the models is not in question, only their insensitivity to the demands of situational pluralism.

It is apparent that transracial communication lacks a diagrammatical model sufficient for adequate picturing of the complexities of the transaction between persons of different ethnic backgrounds. Barnlund has spoken of the model's value as the ease with which it handles a multitude of variables and relates their effects upon each other in highly complicated ways, thus preserving the integrity of events under study.[8] Equally important is the heuristic advantage of the model, which points the way with great transparency to new formulations, theoretical approaches, and assumptions. I have included a cryptic form of transracial communication in a later chapter.

## PURPOSE

Several answers could be given to the question, What is the purpose of transracial communication anyway? All

[7]The two other models that specifically come to mind are Bruce H. Westley and Malcolm S. MacLean, Jr., "A Conceptual Model for Communicating Research," *Journalism Quarterly*, 34 (1957), 31–38, and Theodore M. Newcomb, "An Approach to the Study of Communicative Acts," *Psychological Review*, 60 (1953), 393–404.

[8]Barnlund, "Transactional Model," p. 86.

these answers relate to some basic reasons for any kind of communication.

The first is that communicators usually want a shared meaning elicited from the secondary initiator. Both meaning and understanding are involved in this communication aim. Inasmuch as meaning is the coming together of experiences, it is aroused in the secondary initiator by provocation of the primary initiator. When another person understands our structured experiences, meaning has been aroused in him. To understand presupposes shared experience; to misunderstand is failure to share experience. The quest for communication, then, is an attempt to relate to other human beings. Harmonious human relationships are necessary for maintaining a sane society and psychical stability within the individual.

And because the hallmark of human society is shared experiences and meanings, persons unable to arouse shared meanings within others are considered abnormal. Occasionally a tragic error is made because of this fact. For example: After a few drinks, a Russian immigrant managed to get picked up by the authorities of an eastern state. Unable to understand what the man was saying, the officers had him sent to a mental institution. Thirty-five years later, a physician who understood Russian and happened to be examining the patient discovered that the man was sane. The immigrant had finally met someone with whom he could share meaning! He was immediately released. The ability to arouse meaning in others is one indication of our value to other human beings.

In transracial contexts, a person unable to arouse shared meaning in one of another race over a given period of time might conceivably dismiss the other person as "out of his mind," "crazy," or some similar expression.

The folklore of the South is rich with stories of the "crazy nigger" or "big bad black," who, according to the legends, lived beyond the fear of evil whites because they thought he was insane. Arrogant when he was supposed to be humble, forceful when he was supposed to be submissive, and violent when he was supposed to be religious, this kind of black man upset the experiences of the whites. In still another sense, blacks viewing white politicians or white activists might refer to their language and action as "crazy." It is not uncommon for blacks to contend that "whites are mad" when recalling incidents involving whites and minority people. This is possible because the signs and symbols used by one ethnic group may not arouse shared meanings within another group. Thus, one answer to the question of why we should have effective transracial communication is the possibility of shared meanings and experiences that make for a more orderly society.

A second answer to such a question takes its cue from the first answer. To speak of shared meanings and experiences is to say something about how humans relate to each other now, and what the possibilities are for more effective relationships later. As far as transracial communication is concerned, there is certainly a need for the various racial groups within a society to relate. Societies are best ordered by meaningful exchange and interchange of thoughts and ideas. Therefore, to understand the nature of conflict as expressed in symbols and signs between people of different races is to open the door for interactive effectiveness. Understanding how we relate, of course, is only one part of fulfilling our purpose. With the understanding of the nature of the problem, we must insist upon ways to correct previous behavior. In this fashion we move from where we are to where we want to be in transracial communication. It is one thing for me to analyze my failure to relate meaningfully with you through symbolic verbal interaction; it is another thing for me to correct faulty behavior for more productive interaction in the future. Thus, how we understand the person of another race and how we respond to his symbols and signs tell us something about how we relate to that individual. During this process we can also monitor our behavior in order to correct the faulty linkage.

Third, transracial communication is a method of tension reduction between persons of different races. We tend to have more tension in strange interactional situations than we do in familiar surroundings, with friends, speaking on subjects that are mutually interesting. Race differences, unfortunately, can increase individual tension in the already strange setting, and the ability to engage in meaningful communicative behavior with a person of another race is one way to decrease tensions. Tensions result because of anxieties, and anxieties exist when we do not know what to expect from unknown situations. Many people, operating on hearsay, old people's fables, and community customs, harbor unfounded fears that can lead to irrational behavior in transracial contexts. It is true, too, that the rabid racist may consider the ability to communicate transracially as wasted talent. At the worst, interactional situations can degenerate into tension-creating events. Luckily, such occasions do not occur often when serious communicators are involved in verbal interaction. All human communication must begin from the acceptance of the other person's fundamental humanness. Once this is accomplished, the participants view each other in terms of needs and desires, and discover that they are more alike than not. Thus, a primary purpose in transracial communication centers on minimizing the inconsistencies that produce tension in interpersonal relations.

In addition, interpersonal communication within transracial contexts reduces tension by providing us with concrete information about other people. But do not be misled by this statement. The fact that you interacted with a person of another race should not be taken by you as an indication of your knowledge of people of that race. To judge other members of a racial or ethnic group by the one person you interacted with is another kind of prejudging. The person you met might conceivably be intelligent, articulate, and magnanimous, but that gives you little reason to balloon that interaction to mean more than it does. Once concrete information is experienced through interpersonal communication, one might exclaim, "I never knew you were like this," or, "I had a wrong impression about you." Both these responses, while not the reactions of normal communication, indicate a basic humility needed to ease tensions. When a person is able to say, "I do not know all your perspectives, but I am willing to be shown," or, "My interracial communication is a little rusty from inaction, but I am interested in meaningful interaction," then the tension-reducing process has begun.

Both Berlo and Miller recognized the significance of the communicators' status to interpersonal communication.[9] We can assume that when two persons interact face-to-face, one or the other will perceive himself as

[9]See David K. Berlo, *The Process of Communication* (New York: Holt, Rinehart & Winston, Inc., 1960); and George A. Miller, *Language and Communication* (New York: McGraw-Hill Book Company, 1951).

"superior to" or "more powerful than" the other person. Because there is a tendency for individuals to "size up" their counterparts, this will occur in transracial communication. Some communicators *assume* higher status than the person with whom they are communicating. When people come into contact with each other, it is often easy for one to assume a high- or low-status position in relation to the other. This is a particularly significant aspect of transracial interaction and must be viewed as an area needing understanding. This self-conception vis-à-vis the other is determined by *immediate* and *distant* influential factors.

Immediate factors are those social qualities initially perceived when two persons come into contact with each other—that is, qualities assumed by each from the general appearance and demeanor of the other. Distant factors are those influences and qualities not clearly perceivable on the basis of a physical meeting; these include qualities of intellect and personality, which might become manifest during a communication transaction, as well as preconceived notions about the ethnic group of which the other person is a member. Thus, when two persons of different ethnic backgrounds interact, they assume status positions derived from their own self-concept in combination with *immediate* and *distant* influential factors.

Impressions can often change dramatically during conversation when one communicator learns that the other person is of a low-status ethnic group, even though the initial meeting may have been pleasant. The communicator with preconceived notions about other ethnic groups, upon learning of the other's identity, may adjust his communicative approach to the other person. Two experiences will serve to illustrate the situation.

A few years ago, a teacher with most of the characteristics of a Caucasian got a position in a California high school. She was an excellent teacher, and no one at the predominantly white school gave or expressed a thought about the possibility of her being of any other race. One day, however, during a heated discussion on fair housing, she said "As a black woman, I feel that we must protect the right of every person to own or rent a home anyplace he wants." Her colleagues sat back in stunned silence; they did not expect one so close to their ranks to reveal a fact so powerful in their midst. Afterwards she was treated with great coolness, as one who had been infected with the plague. Efforts to communicate now had an additional element—she was black—and her fellow teachers began to converse with her on a different basis. Eventually, she became the sociologist, economist, and commentator on all black-related events. Heretofore she had merely given her opinion like the others; but now a special relationship developed between her and the other teachers, and whatever communication occurred was with this new perspective.

While blacks, as well as other ethnic groups, will undoubtedly bring to the communication situation certain unique views, to accept this as a distinguishing mark of all members of an ethnic group, on every occasion, is to be grossly mistaken as to what transracial communication is about. Although it does not seek to strip anyone of his ethnicity, it does seek to normalize the communication process so that "who you are does not get in the way of what you say."

Of course, your personality and mannerisms will be a part of the communicated message, but effective transracial communication minimizes the variable of race. In other examples where communicators adjust their messages as the receiver's identity emerges, the absurdity of allowing race to affect communication is underlined. A prominent Mexican-American sought to buy a house in a Texas community. He informed a real estate agent by phone that he had just arrived in town and was interested in purchasing a house listed by the firm; the agent agreed to show it to him. Upon his arrival, the gentleman was told that a mistake had been made: "We expected a Spaniard from Spain."

Admittedly, these examples are crude. But so is the stuff of which they are made—prejudgment of others on the basis of race.

# three

# *CULTURE AND TRANSRACIAL COMMUNICATION*

# Objectives

AFTER READING THIS CHAPTER, YOU SHOULD BE ABLE
TO:

1. Discuss with others the elusiveness of a concept of culture.
2. Provide in writing a discussion of the author's special view of culture.
3. Describe how time can be viewed differently by various peoples.
4. List in writing several expressions that point to the "commercialization" of time in Western societies.
5. Give your own definition of culture.
6. List the two currents operating in the "hang-loose" concept of time.
7. Discuss the merit of co-culture as opposed to subculture.
8. Cite some words used among black Americans to indicate physical relationship.
9. Give a historical account of the development of Black English.
10. List several characteristics of Black English.

In this chapter, we shall be concerned with the concept of culture and its relationship to communication within a transracial context. Our particular focus is on the cultural components that affect harmonious trans-racial-communication behavior. We shall also explore the varieties of culture within the American society.

## A VIEWPOINT ON CULTURE

One can probably find scholars who will argue any possible view of culture, and with some validity. Culture, like communication, has fallen heir to a lifetime of defini-tion and redefinition by anthropologists, sociologists, and psychologists. [The view expressed here is that culture represents the manifold ways people see and organize phenomena.] Most usually, cultural grouping is defined as people sharing a common code, heritage, history, and social organization pattern. Cultural reality is expressed in a people's institutions, proverbs, ceremonies, religion, and polity, and can be identified as separate from the culture of another people. For example, to speak of Western culture as opposed to African or Oriental culture is, among other things, to speak of the products of Judeo-Christian religion, Roman law and politics, and the Greek conception of beauty.

But culture is also a way of thinking, and people liv-ing in Western society learn according to Western cultural behavior. This is also true for people of non-Western origin who have been educated and indoctrinated with European ways of thinking. However, residual aspects of a non-Western person's primary cultural background may often be revealed. Thus it is not unusual to find an African professional, educated and indoctrinated with Western religious and philosophical concepts, relying upon his tribal doctors when he is sick or calling upon the overt God of Africa, "Olorun," "Bon Dieu," or "Abasi," in times of insecurity and depression. To a lesser degree, persons with no immediate contact in the past with the culture of their origin are often found to have a way of thinking that was developed within a close-knit society of their own. Hence, black Americans have evolved certain language and other behavior characteristics that constitute a co-cultural manifestation. Bascom and Herskovits have pointed out that despite the harsh conditions of acculturation under slavery, African religions have been able to flourish in an industrialized, cosmopolitan, and urban life.[1]

Men in all societies respond to the same realities. The perception of those realities, however, manifests itself in various manners. In fact, to say that we all react to the same concrete realities might not be exactly correct, because what one person perceives when focusing on a given phenomenon might be different from another's perception. Only in the sense that all men live in the same concrete world and must react to the same phenomena can we say that all persons respond to the same realities.

[1]William Bascom and Melville Herskovits, *African Cultures* (Chicago: University of Chicago Press, 1959), p. 4.

As we shall see in a later chapter, our peculiar perspectives on reality can affect transracial communication. Each person brings to the interpersonal relationship, as with other realities, a store of ideas, beliefs, habits, customs, and attitudes significantly different from those of other people. As people differ, individually and culturally, in their orientation to given realities, congruence on any phenomenon is difficult.[2] Church has argued that cultures differ in their structural homogeneity and heterogeneity.[3] Less technological societies tend to produce people who share the same basic assumptions about reality, while advanced societies manifest more division on basic issues. Support for this view has been expressed by Jahn in his analysis of traditional African culture.[4] He explains that in traditional African culture, it is not possible to separate theology from medicine or vice versa without violating the entire world view. However, as more Africans come into contact with other cultures, new interpretations will emerge, giving rise to the same kind of diversity present within Western society, and endangering phenomenal perceptual congruence.

Culture, above all, is what distinguishes human beings from the rest of the animal universe. Of all beings in the biological world, only man creates and uses language propositionally, possesses religion, appreciates art, and manufactures instruments of construction and destruction. These are learned and shared behaviors, and

[2]Joseph Church, *Language and the Discovery of Reality* (New York: Vintage Books, Random House, Inc., 1961), p. 138.
[3]*Ibid.*
[4]Janheinz Jahn, *Muntu: An Outline of Neo-African Culture* (New York: Grove Press, Inc., 1961), *passim.*

any behavior that is learned and shared is cultural, from making an arrowhead and tying one's shoelaces to believing and denying.] Culture, therefore, is not instinctive or biologically determined, as is the case with behavior among subhuman animal forms. We learn to view phenomena as others in our group have done; we tend to behave in given situations as we have learned from others to behave. Indeed, the process of teaching is a form of cultural learning and sharing mediated by symbols.

[Transracially, problems of communication are often seriously aggravated by the incongruence of cultural experiences. This is not to say that communicators must possess identical world views before they can have meaningful discussion; it is rather to argue that shared cultural influences and experiences among communicators produce more predictable results.] As it would be extremely difficult for me to understand a physicist explaining the theory of relativity—not because of any lack of intelligence on either of our parts, but because of the technical language and esoteric nature of his explanation—so it is with any communicators possessing different coding systems. Of course, were I a physicist listening to a physicist, the theory of relativity might make better sense to me. Let me emphasize here that people who share similar cultural backgrounds also have communication problems. It is simply my assumption that people who have learned and shared the same culture will have a higher probability of understanding each other than if they had different code and behavior characteristics.

Our culture influences and our communication patterning help to determine the characteristics of our struc-

[5]Alfred G. Smith, *Communication and Culture* (New York: Holt, Rinehart & Winston, Inc., 1966), p. 7.

turizations. In an investigation reported by Ronald Lippitt and Ralph K. White, Kurt Lewin studied experimentally created social "climates" and discovered that human interaction was affected by cultural context.[6] In an elemental sense, we can observe the effect on our own interpersonal behavior when we are with friends, strangers, or relatives. Although this type of contextual influence is not of the same mold as culture in the large, it is illustrative of the influence of different structural characteristics of interactive situations. Lewin studied the experimentally created contexts of democratic, authoritarian, and laissez-faire situations, but the results of the experiment, like our casual observation, showed that we are creatures of context.

Demonstrative studies have been made on cultural differences and communication by several scholars. Eisenstadt investigated the communication processes among immigrants in Israel and found that some important differences existed between the structuring of the communicative function of North African and European Jews.[7] In 1958, Bennett and McKnight examined interpersonal relations among Japanese in America.[8] They developed a cultural model of interaction with several categories from the Japanese interpersonal norms. Following Ruth Benedict's lead, they identified several general features of the

[6]Ronald Lippitt and Ralph K. White, "Patterns of Aggressive Behavior in Experimentally Created Social Climates," *Journal of Social Psychology*, 10 (1939), 271–99.

[7]Shmuel Noah Eisenstadt, "Communication Processes Among Immigrants in Israel," *Public Opinion Quarterly*, 16 (1952), 42–58.

[8]See John Bennett and Robert K. McKnight, "Social Norms, Imagery and Interpersonal Relations," in John Bennett, Herbert Passin, and Robert K. McKnight, *In Search of Identity: The Japanese Overseas Scholar in America and Japan* (Minneapolis: University of Minnesota Press, 1958), pp. 225–39.

Japanese norm, among which were articulate codification of rules, primary associative qualities, hierarchy, concern for status, relative permanence of status, and behavioral reserve and discipline. Such studies tend to identify certain concepts for intercultural communication on the international level, and to provide a rationale for cross-cultural communication between diplomats and statesmen. Although significant, these studies of culture and communication are scarcely concerned with the cross-cultural dimension that can be viewed intranationally.

A multiethnic nation is also a nation of several cultures, and therefore communication may well be across cultural lines even when, because we have been educated to perceive a homogeneous society, we think it is not. Although blacks comprise the largest single minority group in America, there are millions of Mexican-Americans in the Southwest, thousands of Asian-Americans, and numerous American Indians, plus other distinct ethnic groups. Communication between these groups and the larger white society is the greatest barrier to multiethnic harmony. Unable to view the problem as cultural, the white society may often wonder what is wrong with plain American English that blacks, chicanos, and other groups cannot accept it. Of course there may be nothing wrong with the white person's language, or for that matter with the minority person's; they could conceivably be on different wavelengths because of cultural dissimilarity.

## TIME

Edward Hall says that time speaks more plainly than words and is subject to less distortion than spoken language.[9] How we approach time says a lot about our interpersonal communication. Furthermore, it is difficult to conceal our conception of time. Most Americans have a highly commercial concept of time. On the other hand, black Americans tend to have a more "hang-loose" attitude toward it. Because of these differences, transracial communication between blacks and whites often demands that the participants in interpersonal interactions understand each other's special perspective on time.

The commercial concept of time is most prevalent in American society. Unquestionably, there are many coculture people who have accepted this commercial perspective. It is not unusual for people within this society to suggest by language usage their high premium on temporality. Thus, when someone is behind schedule, he seeks to "make time," and in this connection time becomes a commodity to be appropriated for his particular use. There is also the suggestion that one can "lose time," something no one wants to do. But if you "lose time," you might try to "buy time" by engaging in "time-saving" activities; even the supermarkets advertise products as "time-savers" as well as "wife-savers." And then there are the careless people who "waste time" as the frivolous waste money. Clearly our language is replete with commercial references to time.

Time can be treated cavalierly among Americans of non-European origin. Black Americans are familiar with the many "African People's Time" jokes. But to say that blacks have a traditionally "hang-loose" attitude toward time is not to make a judgment about the value of conforming to the general American conception of it. The

[9]Edward T. Hall, *The Silent Language* (New York: Doubleday & Company, Inc., 1959; Fawcett Books, 1961), p. 15.

distinctions of one concept of time are not more correct or more right than those of another. Each has its basis and its utility.

Hall illustrates the time differential between American Indians and white Americans by telling of a Christmas dance he attended at a church in an Indian pueblo near the Rio Grande. He arrived at one o'clock in the wintry morning, but the dance had not yet begun. Many minutes passed, and one of the few whites who had gathered for the dance said, "There is no way of telling when they will start. Last year, I heard, they started at ten o'clock." When an Indian entered the church and poked up the fire in the stove, the whites thought the dance would begin. But another hour passed, and another Indian entered the consistory and disappeared through the door at the nave. Then suddenly, just as the whites were almost exhausted, the dance began.[10]

Among black Americans, one can see a similar attitude toward time when it comes to recreation and fun. A colleague of mine at a university threw a big dance party for twenty or twenty-five couples, whites and blacks. The party had been announced for nine o'clock in the evening, but a very interesting situation began developing. By 9:30, most of the whites had shown up, but only one black couple had appeared. The host and hostess began wondering if the blacks were boycotting the party; after all, there had been much talk in the air about integration and separation. One or two more black couples arrived by ten o'clock; by this time, all the invited whites were present. Whites began to talk in small voices about the absence of black faculty members at the

[10]*Ibid.*, pp. 21–22.

party, and another hour passed. Around 11:15, the party took on a markedly changed complexion, and by midnight, when some whites were thinking of leaving, the party had begun in earnest. Interestingly enough, those blacks who arrived late made no effort to apologize; they had simply been operating on "A. P." (African People's) time.

Another example of this "hang-loose" concept of time occurred a few years ago, when a pregnant Nigerian mother was given a baby shower by one of her Afro-American friends. In this instance, only one white person had been invited; the remainder of the guests were black. Invitations had requested the guests' presence at six o'clock in the evening. When six o'clock arrived, only the white girl and the hostess were at the shower. Engaging in light conversation, the hostess and guest tried to find something to do while they waited. Around 6:30, the guest of honor phoned to say she would be a little late because she had stopped to pick up a prescription at the pharmacy. At seven o'clock, the black guests had begun to arrive, and at 7:30, the guest of honor appeared. The shower was a success for friendships and the expected baby. The guests who felt the urge to explain said things like, "I had to feed the family," "My mother wanted to come, so I gave her a ride," and "My neighbor wanted me to drive her to the store just as I was to leave." Other guests felt no need to explain, primarily because there are two sides to the "hang-loose" concept of time. One is definitely humanistic; the other has to do with the grand entrances. To appear on time is an indication of low status, particularly for a festive event such as a baby shower. To receive the attention of others, one must arrive after their arrival. So two currents operate in the "hang-loose" concept: (1) Priority belongs to the significant work I am now doing, and (2) only low-status persons attend festive events according to the announced time.

Misunderstandings in transracial communication can often occur when whites, possessing a commercial concept of time, encounter a black person whose cavalier attitude about time transcends the boundaries of recreation to those more sacred sectors of our society. Unable to see why there should be any cultural differences in our distinctions of time, the white person is liable to speak of the black person as irresponsible. On the other hand, black people often have a higher premium upon quality than efficiency. Evidence of this can be seen in life-style as well as in literature about blacks. It is often inconceivable to whites that blacks barely above the poverty level would want to drive secondhand Chryslers and Cadillacs. But such cars, even if they do not function properly, still represent the appearance of quality. However, this is another argument. The point to be made here is that blacks would much rather perform well than perform on time. Priorities in the home or community might well keep a black person from keeping an appointment with an important businessman. There is in this cultural concept of time something of what black writers have referred to as a humanistic approach to life.[11] Of course, both blacks and whites need to understand each other's concept of time if communication insensitivity is to be avoided.

[11]The artistic and literary works of persons such as Imamu Baraka, Nikki Giovanni, Don Lee, and Asafo attest to the humanistic approach to life. They argue that blacks are inclined toward humanism in art, politics, religion, and interpersonal relations. See Vernon Dixon and Badi Foster, *Beyond Black or White* (Boston: Little, Brown and Company, 1971), pp. 7–22.

34

But time is only one dimension of the cultural differences that exist among American people intranationally. Let us now turn to another dimension of American culture, with an eye toward the understanding that is the substance of communication.

## FAMILY

It has often been argued by persons of various social, religious, and political persuasions that the family is the basic unit of our institutions; in fact, the argument establishes the family as the smallest institution within the society. This view is held by most Americans, whether black, yellow, brown, or white. However, while the family is generally perceived as the basic unit in American society, *what constitutes the family varies from group to group.*

Blacks tend to have a more extended concept of the family than do whites. This is evident on several different levels of interaction in the black community. Consider the elaborate use of the terms "brother" and "sister," which indicate a filial relationship between black people. To be a "brother" or "sister" is to share with the communicator a special relationship to the world.

As the family unit stands in a unique relationship to society's other institutions, so the extended family of the black person is a unit conceived in uniqueness. Thus, when blacks meet each other, the greeting is often, "How's it going, brother," "Stick in there, sister," or a similar expression showing one person's closeness to another. The communicator and respondent perceive the special relationship, and in discussion with a third party about the meeting, both might indicate this common bond by another word. Merely giving a narrative, one of the participants in the interactive event where "brother" or "sister" was used might say to a third party, "I met this blood today who had just come from Vietnam." "Blood" sends the same message as "brother" and "sister," while at the same time placing a consanguineous quality on the relationship. Other contemporary terms used to refer to other blacks are "skin" and "member," again demonstrating the kinship.

At another level, the term "mother" can be used to indicate the special place an older woman within the black community has come to hold. There are "mothers of the church," "community mothers," and other women with "Mother" attached to their names by respectful members of the community. As an extension of one's own family, the black person sees others as his brothers, sisters, mothers, and even occasionally fathers. Such a conception of family is difficult to find within the white community. Thus, in transracial communication, when the nonblack communicator understands the nature of the black man's family, more valid conclusions can be drawn about black life and values. To be black in America is to have the largest family in the world, because it is quite literally possible that the other black person is your brother or sister.[12]

## BLACK LANGUAGE STYLES

In recent years there has been a growing interest in Black English. What is the origin of Black English? Who speaks

[12]William H. Grier and Price M. Cobbs, *Black Rage* (New York: Basic Books, Inc., 1968), *passim*.

it? And what are its implications for transracial interactions involving speakers of Black English?

The beginnings of Black English are found in the initial contact between West African languages and English. Speakers of the African languages of Efik, Yoruba, Ibo, Mande, Twi, and others, who were introduced to the vocabulary and grammatical constructions of English, devised a language that, while functional, retained certain Africanisms. The basic elements in a language are vocabulary and grammar, and more often than not, Black English borrowed English vocabulary and retained African grammatical elements. Actually, a considerable number of African words were also retained in Black English. In Geechee and Gullah, variant forms of Black English spoken along the coasts of South Carolina and Georgia, several thousand words have been demonstrated as having African origin.[13] There are also a number of words commonly thought of as American English that have African origin. Among these are *okra, samba, goober*, and *biddy*.

Black English cannot properly be called incorrect English. It has its own regularized grammar and a predictable grammatical pattern; this is an important key to communication with those who speak it. Over a hundred years ago in a Geechee community, a teacher had such difficulty getting the children to reply to simple questions that he had decided to resign and return to the North. But when the father of one of his students came to the class and watched a demonstration of the teacher's method, it was clear to the father that the method was incorrect. The teacher had asked the class, "What color is the sky?" No one had responded. The father asked his son, "How sky stun?" The whole class responded with a

[13]Lorenzo Turner, *Africanisms in the Gullah Dialect* (Chicago: University of Chicago Press, 1949).

loud "Blue!" Teachers seeking to improve their ability to communicate with pupils who speak Black English would do well to learn the grammatical interference points.

Black English regularly treats the conjugated form of the verb *to be* as understood. Thus, *am, is,* and *are* are typically omitted in Black English, so that the sentence, "John is at home," would be said, "John, he at home"; and "She is running" would be said, "she running." If a person was responding to the question, "Where is your father working?" he would reply, "He be working. . . ."

Black English also has different rules for plurals. The sentence, "Mary has ten sisters," would be rendered as "Mary have ten sister" in Black English. The system does not require a pluralization of "sister" when some other word within the sentence indicates pluralization; to say "Mary has ten sisters" would be grammatical redundancy. Also note that in the Black English sentence, there appears to be inconsistency between the subject and verb: "Mary have. . . ." However, if the subject were plural, the verb would remain the same.

Teachers could exert much more influence on their black pupils by treating Black English as a foreign language. English could be learned as a second language; there is nothing to indicate that proficiency in Black English would minimize one's proficiency in English, or vice versa. Students who speak Spanish do not have to be told to forget Spanish in order to acquire English; in fact, a person's ability to communicate is enhanced if he knows two languages.

All black Americans do not speak Black English; some speak English and some speak incorrect English. One is most likely to find Black English spoken in the Southern coastal states and in the urban areas frequented

by Southern blacks. Of course, there are regional variations as there are of other languages. The important variations tend to be in vocabulary; thus, "hawk" is used in
Chicago for the howling wintry cold, and "eagle" is used
in Seattle for payday, but the terms are not necessarily
common, say, in Dallas.

The transracial communicator who views Black English as a legitimate code spoken by several million people, notwithstanding the importance of learning English,
is likely to attain greater satisfaction from communication
with speakers of Black English than are those who see the
language as negative.

## Black Idioms

Most people find it difficult to "get through" to people who speak a different language. We use hand gestures, facial contortions, and other physical movements
when we need to communicate with someone who
understands only a little English. If you have been to a
foreign country and have tried to communicate in a language you barely understood, you have recognized this
phenomenon.

Because blacks have lived in America for a long time
(actually here before the *Mayflower*), many words and
expressions are a part of our common language. Still others are easy to understand. When a black person says,
"J. T. is talking to Mary," instead of, "J. T. is going steady
with Mary," he is resorting to the language of the community. The nonblack who understands this and is able
to incorporate a few of these expressions into his own
vocabulary will certainly indicate his ability to communicate. Similarly, a black person who incorporates into his

language the use of regular English expressions demonstrates his ability to grasp what others say. To understand that when a black person says of another, "Man, she's together," he means that the person is in control of her activities, whether intellectual or social, is to sense the liveliness of the language. These idioms can frequently lead to misunderstandings. Such was the case in California a few years ago, when a black student was placed on the witness stand as a defendant to testify about the murder of one of his friends. In the narrative dealing with the last time he saw his friend, the student said, "I was really coming down hard on him, we were in the thick of things, so I had to come down hard on him to make him understand." The white prosecuting attorney felt content he had shown that the defendant was guilty. But "coming down hard" was subsequently pointed out to the court to be an expression often used to indicate intense conversation.

"Getting through" is a mutual undertaking for the speakers of different languages. The best procedure is to listen as carefully as possible to the language, making certain not to lose the chance to ask for information regarding what you do not understand. The psychological climate improves when we understand why people speak as they do, that a language system is different does not mean it is deficient.

## Black Slang

Black Slang represents the words and expressions most recently created by black Americans to convey meaning and purpose. Usually the slang word is closely related to the conventional word. Thus, "car" becomes "ride," or "knife" becomes "blade." The expressions that follow are typical slang expressions of recent origin.

| Expressions | Translations |
|---|---|
| Ain't it funky now | It is a good situation |
| He's bogarting | He's using force |
| It's ass-kicking time | It's time to fight |
| We had to haul ass | We had to run |
| Check it out | See if it's right |

| Words | Translations |
|---|---|
| Hype | Steal |
| Bitch | To argue |
| Mean | Really good-looking |
| Mellow | Delightful |
| A. P. T. | African People's Time |
| Set | Party |
| Split | To leave |
| Wheels | Car |

This list is merely suggestive of the numerous words and expressions that are prevalent among blacks. Use of these expressions in the Black English syntax can frequently be confusing for those who are unaware of the extent of Black Slang and Black English. In addition to the vocabulary and grammatical forms, there are language functions that aid in understanding what is being communicated.

## FUNCTIONS OF BLACK LANGUAGE

Thomas Kochman has identified several words that refer to special ways of talking: *rapping, shucking, jiving, running it down, gripping, copping a plea, signifying,* and *sounding.*[14] These terms refer to language functions and

[14]Thomas Kochman, "Toward an Ethnography of Black American Speech Behavior," in Arthur L. Smith, *Language, Communication and Rhetoric in Black America* (New York: Harper & Row, Publishers, 1972), pp. 58–86.

may incorporate characteristics of Black English or Black Slang.

*Rapping* is the use of colorful language to present some controversial narrative. There has to be at least one other possible position to that of the rapper. The rapper makes his case on the strength of facts plus enthusiastic and lively conversation.

*Shucking* refers to the language function characterized by any stylistic artifice employed to appear acceptable. It is the form frequently used to talk oneself out of a troublesome situation. *Jiving* is often used in connection with *shucking*. The meaning usually conveyed is *lying*.

*Running it down* is a form of communicating facts, opinions, beliefs, and advice. The preacher "runs down" the scriptures on charity and hope, for example; or the pimp could be "running down" the figures on the latest deals.

*Copping a plea* functions as a language tactic to extricate oneself from an embarrassing position. If you are in trouble with someone stronger than yourself, you "cop a plea." A person may "cop a plea" by explaining that he did not mean to cause anyone harm with his actions, or that he was forced to do what he did, etc.

*Signifying* and *sounding* can be considered together because they both refer to verbal insult. The game called "the dozens" is often the basis of *sounding, signifying*, or *screaming*, as this lively game of repartee is called. "The dozens" are rhymed insults usually directed at a person's relatives, particularly his mother.

Blacks who have grown up in urban ghetto areas or in certain rural regions have always used special phrases, words, or expressions. Psychological survival often depended upon one's ability to "play the dozens" or to "shuck" when necessary or to "run the stuff down" to the cats who asked for the information. Understanding of the uniqueness of black language styles can help in bridging the communication gaps in American society.

## AN APPROACH TO INTERVENTION

When the communication process is modified in order to facilitate a relaxed, unstrained interaction between transracial communicators, the modifying factor is called intervention. It is an interference of the tensed and strained process of communication that usually involves misunderstandings.

Effective interventions must rely upon several conventional principles of human communication. To do otherwise is to prescribe without an adequate diagnosis of why persons experience difficulty in communication. Listening is the most underrated activity in human communication. Most of us have been made aware of the kinds of things to say in argument, in discussion, and in discourse; how to listen has not been as thoroughly treated. Consequently, comments such as "he's a good talker," or, "she sure is articulate" are heard with regularity, while comparatively few persons are described as good listeners. Talking is one essential component of communication; listening is the other.

Therefore, as James Winans, a pioneer in speech communication, frequently observed, when we give attention to messages from others, we indicate our interest. A prominent theme in the weekly ritual of mass meetings led by the Reverend Jesse Jackson of Operation Breadbasket is "I am somebody." By listening to another, we affirm his concept of himself while acquiring specific information. Interest, then, is demonstrated by what is called attentive or active listening. In fact, all listening should be attentive and active. Listening is not a static function; and it is its dynamism that differentiates it from undefined hearing.

In transracial communication, because the communicators will usually have dissimilar backgrounds and experiences, listening will have to involve a conscious effort to "read into" the other person. This "reading into" should be based upon our knowledge of ethnic and cultural factors that might contribute to perception and the formulation of ideas.

Another principle of human communication is that the communicators must make themselves available to each other. Chicano and black communicators, as well as other transethnic configurations, demand availability. In terms of communication, availability must include both proximity and willingness; that is, the communicators must make themselves mentally as well as physically available. Physical availability is frequently taken to mean that a communicator is willing to use a telephone or some other message-conveying instrument. Fundamentally, however, when people must talk to each other in head-to-head situations, they should be in each other's presence. Those in our society who have been concerned about the quality of transracial interactions have often argued for open-housing legislation as a way to bring people together. Such a solution, while suggesting a social procedure, also addresses the primary issue that persons who never meet Puerto Ricans or Japanese will not learn how to communicate with them.

Recognition of ethnic similarities and dissimilarities is like recognition of individual similarities and dissimilarities. When we know that our friend Carlos Hernandez is a different individual from Juan Castillo, or that Ayuko Bambako is not the same person in temperament as Ojekan Wale, we have captured the essence of communicative intervention. Individuals are different, and so are ethnic and cultural groupings.

In summary, intervention is a modification of communication behavior. It occurs when communicators listen and anticipate similarities and dissimilarities. Listening is the key concept upon which intervention turns, and we can say with certainty that communication difficulties cannot be solved without the triggering intervention of listening. Thus, intervention relies on conventional processes for modifying interpersonal communication.

**four**

# STRUCTURE
# OF
# TRANSRACIAL
# COMMUNICATION

# Objectives

AFTER READING THIS CHAPTER, YOU SHOULD BE ABLE
TO:

1. *Define in writing what is meant by* structure.
2. *Discuss dyadic and mass communication.*
3. *Discuss how structurizations can be controlled in
   transracial communication by reinforcements.*
4. *List some qualities that affect transracial communication.*
5. *Describe in writing what you understand by task
   appreciation in transracial communication.*
6. *Define normalization by providing some of its
   characteristics in transracial communication.*
7. *Explain the principle of social-symbol reproducibility.*

# FORM AND CONTENT

Transracial communication, like all communication, is manifest as both form and content. And the constraints upon the communication in other dimensions are also a transracial communication. There are a limited number of structural possibilities with communication. The more important ones can be included under the broad headings of *interpersonal* and *mass*. As interbehavior based upon verbal interaction, the communication process can manifest itself in dyads, the smallest transactional group, or in the larger, intergroup experience. To speak of structure is also to include what is said; in fact, the *what* helps determine the *how* of interracial communication. But this must not be construed as referring only to the structurization, the form and content in detail, but to the anatomy of the structure in the large. A message—that is, what is specifically and purposely communicated—is structurization; the external anatomy of that message is what we mean by structure.

Human beings engage in more dyadic than mass communication. Whether it is our conversations with immediate family members, messengers, and retail clerks, or our roommate, class officers, professor, or college president, our communication is basically dyadic. There will, of course, be those times when we will give speeches or hear speeches in a mass meeting, and there will also be times when we will interact in groups; but dyadic, one-to-one, communication is the most prevalent form of human interaction.

Transracial contexts do not significantly alter the basic structure of the interchange except when the psychological constraints on the participants create some changes in communication content as a result of our perceptions. In this way, our perceptions, based upon past experiences and external influences, are directly responsible for our structurizations. All communication is colored by perceptions of reality, and if perceptions are built upon stereotypes or other psychological constraints, the communication structurization is affected. When a white person perceives a black person as "inferior," the kind of communication structurization produced by the white person reflects his image of the black. To see the black person as "inferior" means that the communication message will not reveal any egalitarian intentions. Likewise, when police are viewed as "pigs," the structurization will manifest this perception. Language is a product of our culture, experiences, and stereotypes; and no miracles are worked in interracial communication. But we will discuss language more fully in another chapter. For now let us see how the various transracial situations manifest the structure of communication.

Dyadic transracial situations can reveal a complex system of messages and countermessages, and this system increases and decreases in difficulty in proportion to the communicator's willingness to communicate. When two persons of dissimilar ethnic backgrounds engage in conversation, they frequently bring into play patterns of reinforcement or disapproval that aid in controlling each other's communication behavior. It may seem unlikely that our communication activity can be controlled and manipulated by another in a dyadic setting; but in fact, this is what happens in most two-person communication situations. Sometimes we are the manipulated, and sometimes we manipulate. A study has shown that a psychotherapist can control what a patient verbalizes by controlling reinforcement contingencies—that is, by the way the psychotherapist nods his head and gives other signs.[1] In such a case, the patient does not have to know that he is being controlled. Similarly, in two-person communication settings, the communicators control each other, occasionally with one person dominating. But the effectiveness of communication under these circumstances depends in part on the willingness of the parties to engage in transracial communication. A lack of such willingness results in a higher degree of complexity involving messages and countermessages, as the communicators try to outwit or "get the best" of each other. As we know by now, this is not the way to increase interpersonal communication, transracially or otherwise.

## QUALITIES AFFECTING STRUCTURE

### Willingness

The person who engages in interpersonal communication must possess a willingness to communicate, combined with accessibility to the other person. There are some situations that have particular requirements, and interpersonal communication in transracial contexts is one. *Willingness* means that the potential communicator

[1] Leonard Krasner, "Studies of the Conditioning of Verbal Behavior," *Psychological Bulletin*, 55 (1958), 148–70.

is not merely indifferent to the communication event, but is actively interested in what is being communicated by source and message. If we refused to demonstrate willingness to engage in conversation, the prospects for meaningful interaction would be bleak indeed. This is to say that all technical systems—communication channels, cognitive factors and receiving organs—might be functioning properly and yet we would fail to have significant interaction.

To be willing is to be sensitive to other people. Willingness is not applicable merely to transracial communication; it is a cardinal rule of all communication. Parents often have difficulty with sullen children who will not reveal why they are angry. The college student who shares a dormitory room or apartment with another may have frequently found that his roommate "does not want to talk about it." "It" could be of a multitude of things, from a breakup with a lover to a poor grade in communication theory. But in any case, it is clear that the noncommunicative person is unwilling to talk with parents or friends, and at that point lacks the essential sensitivity required for meaningful interaction.

## Accessibility

Implied in willingness is an attempt to become accessible to the other person. Defense mechanisms that prevent one person from interacting with another should be controlled by an active resistance to provincialism. Most defense mechanisms to transracial communication are based upon preconceived notions about the other person. "I don't want to communicate with you because blacks and whites have nothing to talk about," is a commonly held attitude among noncommunicative persons. On the basis of this attitude, avoidance becomes the game of the day in an effort to evade interaction. Clearly, availability is lacking, and no communication can be achieved if we are not accessible to each other. Sometimes past experiences and childhood prejudices color our outlook so that transracial communication is nearly impossible. Seeking to avoid persons of other ethnic or racial groups, some persons have been known to exit by other doors when in an auditorium or to frown when passing a member of another race. These, of course, are extreme cases. Most noncommunicative people simply refuse to become involved in transracial situations by avoiding the schools, stores, neighborhoods, and churches where this cross-cultural interaction is liable to take place.

But anyone seeking transracial communication must become available to the other person. Two persons may have the desire and willingness to communicate but may never do so because they are never available. There are definite limits to how far the human voice can reach, how far the human eye can see, and how far the human ear can detect sound. Such limitations serve to augment the necessity for accessibility between transracial communicators. However, we should not be misled into believing that mere physical proximity means availability. Proximity is only one part of accessibility; the other is the flexibility and sensitivity of the two persons. If they are in proximity and are sensitive to each other in the sense of being able to anticipate responses, attitudes, and judgments, then *availability* exists. It cannot exist in the absence of sensitivity.

Both *willingness* and *availability* are crucial to transracial communication, and as qualities that affect the nature of the structurization, they occupy key positions in this construct of interpersonal communication. What is said is frequently determined by how available the next guy is at a given time; and what is communicated as a message is dependent upon our willingness to accept it. While these may not be the only influences on the trans-racial communicator's message, they are certainly the most critical.

## Task Appreciation

All structurizations reflect specific tasks under consideration by the communicators. In transracial communication, *task appreciation* means an attitude sensitive to the solution or resolution of a given problem involving race or ethnic relations. Sensitivity to each other provides the transracial communications with a measure of problem anticipation, but only under the heat of genuine problems or issues dealing with race can task appreciation be adequately evaluated. In such instances, the communicators must perform together, and performing together is not the same as being sensitive to each other. In performance—that is, joint task resolution or solution —the transracial communicators must deal with a different level of interpersonal relations. Under the pressure of task resolution, they come to do together what they may have doubted they could do before—even if it is to argue honestly and freely.

When two persons of different racial backgrounds engage in serious discussion of an issue related to race, they are likely to create a communicative experience that two persons of the same race never could—or perhaps, never would. Because it is so easy for members of the same ethnic group to agree with each other or to "understand" quickly, if only superficially, what the other person is saying, there is frequently little likelihood of honest interaction. On the other hand, transracial communication tends to involve persons who will take sides aggressively to defend an ethnic perspective and not so easily give it up. In addition, if there is some agreement between the persons of different ethnic backgrounds as they discuss the issue related to race, and if the subject under consideration touches upon the race of one or the other of the communicators, there will still be a strong sense of ethnic responsibility in the agreement with the other person. Persons of similar racial backgrounds tend to dismiss issues related to another race much more lightly than are persons of that race. Therefore, transracial communication produces a new creative experience by giving the communicators an opportunity to become sensitive to the resolution and solution of problems related to race.

## Normalization

In most communication situations, speaker and listener seek to normalize interpersonal relations. Some interactive events are primarily concerned with "crisis" situations; others are more given to casual conversation. But whether the communicators are attempting to arrive at agreement out of a controversy or merely want to interact verbally with each other, normalization is being sought.

In terms of transracial communication, *normalization* means that the communicators are seeking a stage in their interaction where they can appear to each other without affectation. Affectation occurs in much interpersonal communication and is especially detrimental to transracial communication. Sometimes affectation in communication happens almost subconsciously, and at other times it is a planned activity. In both cases, it must be considered an unworthy condition for effective communication.

It is impossible for two persons of different races to communicate in earnest when they're "putting each other on" by acting as if they are honest when in fact they are not. There are many reasons for this kind of action. One might well be that the communicators feel that in order to maintain another person's friendship, or more likely, acquaintance, it is necessary to conceal one's true feelings about pertinent matters. Consider for a moment the communication situation in which a black and a white student are talking about the low demand for Ph.D.'s in physics in today's society. Somewhere in the conversation, the white person refers to the black as "Negro" and then meekly says, "Excuse me, I didn't intend to use that word, it slipped." The white student need not go through the agony of explaining what he meant by the term "Negro." While the term is now held in disfavor by blacks, it does not always call for apologies.

A more vivid example of lack of candor is demonstrated when the black person knowingly responds to political questions put to him in a way pleasing to whites, or when a white person refuses to call a black incompetent because the black may interpret the remark as racial in nature and reply to the white by calling him a racist. Such a situation can, of course, be racial in nature, and many times the communicators may be using their stereotypical impressions, but this is not necessarily so. Both "incompetent" and "racist" are strong words, evoking intense emotional feelings.

Two principles are involved in the process of normalization in transracial communication. The first is the principle of *social-symbol reproducibility*; the second is the principle of *linguistic regularity.* According to the principle of social-symbol reproducibility, whenever persons of different ethnic or racial groups interact verbally, the normalization process occurs in proportion to the length of time they interact. Put another way, the more time persons of different racial or ethnic backgrounds spend in communication with each other, the less difficulty each has in unaffected perception of the other. In addition, this condition is reproducible in any society with two or more ethnic groups. Initial contact between persons of different ethnic backgrounds, especially if they are strangers, mutually sharing negative stereotypes, tends to provoke "sizing up" of each other. While this situation can be reproduced in most societies, the normalization process that occurs with length of communication is also reproducible. I do not suggest that the degree of normalization will be the same in every society. Obviously, lifelong racists would have an extremely difficult time normalizing their communication with persons of the despised or hated race in a one-hour interaction. Indeed, what is being developed here is more significant and more complex than mere talk. Few can doubt that, say, whites and blacks have "talked" to or at each other in some sections of the country for hundreds of years with little or no meaningful changes in racial attitudes. So it is not mere talk that is meant when I argue that normalization occurs in proportion to the length of verbal interaction. To theorize in this manner is not to contend that there will be racial agreement or even racial harmony. As I have indicated, normalization requires that the communicators lose their affected manner.

Now, with the principle of *social-symbol reproducibility* in mind, let us turn to the principle of *linguistic regularity.* In a given dyadic interpersonal-communication situation, certain words that are used are more mutually understandable to both communicators than are others. The word *booty* has several meanings, and in a transracial communication situation between blacks and whites, "Get your booty out of my way" could possibly produce a blind spot for the white listener who was not privy to the word's meaning in the black community. Similarly, a white communicator could conceivably use what to him is an exceptionally common name for a food or household appliance, which might not be understood by his black listener. Much transracial communication rests uneasily on the ladder of mutual linguistic understanding. These difficulties are not inevitable, but we can usually recall one or two instances in our own experience where we wondered what the other person was saying or meaning. The currency of Yiddish words in today's society also leads to a new learning experience, and those who have not grasped the meaning of "chutzpah" can have blind spots in their communication.

Of course, to some extent we all have had occasion to "not know" and yet be able to understand the sense of a statement, sentence, or speech. In fact, while our reading vocabulary is probably more extensive than our speaking vocabulary, there are times when we are not sure of the meaning of a word in a text, yet we understand the paragraph because of context. Needless to say, this situation is constantly being created in interpersonal communication. Our "uh huh's" and shaking heads do not necessarily indicate total understanding of every word uttered; they might merely mean that we understand the drift of what is being said by the speaker. Words can only become "known" to us after we have heard them used and have used them ourselves in various contexts; indeed, the correct use of a word, vocally or written, is a cognitive process.

It is now convenient and possible for us to say that the principle of linguistic regularity contends that the process of normalization in transracial communication occurs more readily in those instances where the communicators regularly share a common language code. In addition, the fewer the linguistic irregularities shared by the communicators, the greater the probability of transracial normalization. Human beings are inclined toward normal relations with those who hold to beliefs, customs, and language habits similar to their own. Therefore, through social-symbol reproducibility and the attempt at linguistic regularity, we minimize differences and accentuate commonalities.

# ✦ five

# A MODEL
# OF
# TRANSRACIAL
# COMMUNICATION

# Objectives

1.  Recite the distinct features that must be accounted for in a communication model.
2.  Describe an initiator.
3.  Describe the universal context.
4.  Describe the ethnic perspective.
5.  Explain how this model differs from other communication models.
6.  Write an essay on the function of models.

The most direct method of presenting the relationships in a transactive communication involving persons of different races is to suggest them by a model. Numerous models—for example, helical, circular, linear —have highlighted the principal aspects of the interpersonal situation by suggesting that communication is process. But to increase understanding of transracial communication, a model must consider other aspects in addition to those traditionally dealt with by communication specialists. Such a model naturally borrows from the work of previous theorists while enlarging upon the scope of the transaction.

There are several distinct features that must be adequately accounted for in a model attempting to clarify the process of transracial communication. First, it must be understood that all communication takes place in the public arena; that is, the transracial communicative reality happens in the world. Thus, a basis of our model is human society, and all else derives from this fact. And human society is composed of all kinds of people, with different heritages, backgrounds, and cultures. It is, in fact, multiethnic. Making harmony out of such diversity is the task of communication, not in the sense that communication takes charge without our wills, but in the more crucial sense that human beings make bonds, contracts, friendships, foes, and love through spoken symbolic interaction. Whatever is accomplished or not accomplished in human relationships can often be traced to verbal linkages. It is no small thing to say that the society is complex and diverse, for in so saying we testify to the immensity of the communicative task. And as a result of the diversity, different ethnic groups see themselves in a certain light and view their aspirations in a certain way. The views and aspirations of one group may be at odds with those of another ethnic group, giving rise to suspicion, tension, and sometimes conflict. The persons who engage in transracial communication tend to view reality from the vantage point of the group. The collective eye of the group often becomes the vision by which the individual sees. Memories, aspirations, complaints, promises, and glories of the group are transferred to the individual communicator, who often unconsciously bears the burdens of his group.

The individual who communicates transracially is what has been called variously *speaker* and *source*. At the beginning point for message verbalizations, the communicator may be called an *initiator*, because he initiates speaking. Of course, messages are affected by the initiator's beliefs, attitudes, and values (BAV). As a source, the person draws upon his experiences and knowledge, as well as his BAV, to construct a message that is manifest in verbal and nonverbal behavior. Finally, perhaps the most important aspect of this transracial communication model is its consideration of a threshold for communication normalization, which is a significant concept in human interaction. Because in transracial communication most human beings tend to be cautious, it is necessary to discuss the impact of this concept on the communicative phenomenon. With this rather general sketch, let us turn to a more in-depth discussion of these ideas.

## Universal Context Of Communication

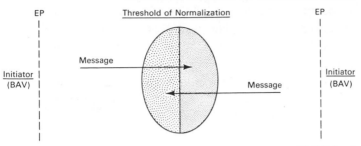

*FIGURE 1*

*This diagrammatical representation shows that the threshold for normalization is flexible depending upon the sensitivities of the transracial communicators.*

# UNIVERSAL CONTEXT

Theoretically, communicators have everything available in the world for their use in human communication. That is, the failures and accomplishments of previous generations, the written record of past civilizations, habits, customs, beliefs, arguments, and experiences of others before and within our time are the special materials from which we create our communication. Simply put, we have the abundant history of humans interacting to provide us with ideas in transracial communication.

In a dyadic communication, as in all types of communication, the participants are in the universal context (UC). Thus, what is available to one communicator is theoretically available to the other. The UC exists neutrally, and can be consulted by any communicator who chooses to explore the possibilities within his mental group. In a sense, it is proper to speak of the UC as deterministic as long as it is understood that no one person ever masters the potentials of the UC. Briefly, then, what is meant by the deterministic nature of the UC is the fact that no person can ever get beyond it and still have communication with another human being. What we say and how we say it are governed by what is available for us to choose from. And because we are unable to choose what is not so available, we must obviously choose from among the given options.

## ETHNIC PERSPECTIVE

The ethnic perspective is that region of the universal context that has been accepted by a given ethnic group as its special view of reality based upon history, culture, and philosophic perception. In transracial communication, the engagees often express ideas, beliefs, and prejudices growing out of ethnic perspective. Although understanding of this phenomenon is no solution to inadequate meaning transference, it is the beginning of a sensitivity without which most persons would remain indifferent or hostile about transracial communication.

As I have stated above, all communication occurs within the universal context; but further, all communication occurs from some ethnic perspective, and this may or may not have anything to do with anthropological or biological classifications of race. One's ethnic perspective is often as much a matter of feeling and emotion as it is of blood. Indeed, everything that is said proceeds from an ethnic perspective, usually unconsciously but sometimes consciously. In addition, all that we hear enters by way of our ethnic perspective. This is illustrated by an experience similar to many that happen to all of us.

A few months ago, a large supermarket in a well-to-do white residential area of a large city was robbed of $3,000, and the thief escaped. A black man, who happened to be in an ice-cream shop a few yards away immediately after the incident, overheard the shop's owner inquire of a white passerby, "Was the robber from around here?" Such a question, meaningless if taken literally, obviously meant, "Was he black? white? Mexican-American?, etc." Questions similar to this one demonstrate the pervasiveness of ethnic perspective.

# INITIATOR

Verbal communication is initiated by a human being. To make such a statement is to suggest something of the nature of man as well as of interpersonal communication. One of man's several distinguishing marks is his ability to begin and engage in verbal communication. Thoughts conceived and emotions felt may be exposed to another in the form of a verbal structurization, with thought and emotion also highlighting man's unique qualities.

In transracial communication, the engagees are most often alternately initiators of verbal structurizations characterized by information sharing, argumentation, and ritual mutual ego building. Some communicative situations are dominated by one or the other of the engagees, and still other situations find the engagees talking at the same time. Neither of these communication situations dominated by the participants is conducive to effective communication.

Initiators are products of the universal context and their ethnic perspective; that is, to some degree what occurs within the initiator's mind, and subsequently what is produced as communication, reflect the contextual and ethnic influences. An ethnic perspective does not necessarily retard transracial communication; in fact, only when the ethnic perspective is also prejudicial toward other people will communicative normalization fail to take place.

There are several major obstacles to interpersonal interaction that are highlighted in a transracial context. These are elements of beliefs, perceptions, and skills. Often transracial communication involves several interlocking and, on occasion, contradictory systems deriving from the communicators' ethnic backgrounds. Such communication is susceptible to misinterpretations and misunderstandings. But this condition does not have to be permanent or necessarily occur. Human beings can and do have successful transracial interactions. Even so, you will find occasional obstructions strewn in the pathway by yourself or another communicator, or by the society.

# six

# *ELEMENTS*
# *OF*
# *TRANSRACIAL*
# *NOISE*

# Objectives

AFTER READING THIS CHAPTER, YOU SHOULD BE ABLE TO:

1. Give in writing Rokeach's four assumptions of connectedness.
2. Explain how control beliefs affect transracial communication.
3. Define stereotype.
4. Show how stereotyping can influence the fidelity of transracial communication.
5. Describe some incident in your experience when you responded incorrectly or not at all because you misunderstood the message.
6. Demonstrate how inadequate perception can influence transracial communication.
7. Define the idea of race-place.

# CONTROL BELIEFS

We have not chosen to include every gradation of belief in this transracial communication model, because the special category of central beliefs bears more directly upon our concern. Some scholars, notably Milton Rokeach and his students, define several types of belief. They argue that beliefs tend to vary along a central-peripheral dimension.[1] Furthermore, resistance to change is greater in a central belief than in others; and the more central the belief changed, the more it will send repercussions throughout the belief system.

Rokeach provides four defining assumptions of connectedness that in turn will tell whether or not a belief is central.[2] (1) Beliefs directly related to one's own existence in the physical world are assumed to be more functionally connected to other beliefs than are those with less direct concern about one's existence. (2) Beliefs concerning existence and self-identity may be shared or not shared with others. Those shared with others are assumed to have more functional connections with and consequences for other beliefs than are those not shared with others. (3) Many beliefs are learned not by direct encounter with the object of belief, but indirectly, from

[1] Milton Rokeach, *The Open and Closed Mind* (New York: Basic Books, Inc., Publishers, 1960), pp. 39–50.
[2] *Ibid.*

71

reference persons and groups. These are derived beliefs. They are assumed to have fewer functional connections and consequences for other beliefs than are those from which they are derived. (4) Numerous beliefs represent more or less arbitrary matters of taste and are often perceived as such by the individual holding them. Such beliefs are assumed to have relatively fewer functional connections and consequences for other beliefs than are beliefs that do not repress arbitrary matters of taste.

A person's perception of his ethnic or racial group is a central belief. In transracial communication, one of the problems facing the communicators is that of overcoming preconceived notions about one's own, as well as the other person's, ethnic group. When the persons attempting to communicate transcend this barrier, they have achieved a basic goal of transracial communication. Few people are able to change or hold their central beliefs in abeyance. But those who are able to check their central beliefs on race and engage in interpersonal communication have often discovered that their preconceived notions prevent them from accepting other human beings as individuals. As a central belief, the idea of *race-place* or status can become a stumbling block for many persons. But if it is transcended, it will, by virtue of its centrality, cause numerous other changes within a person's belief system. If a person no longer believes that black is superior to white or vice versa, then the questions of housing, marriage, voting, political control, and employment cease to hang on the thin string of skin color or cultural background. Of course, if the centrality of race supremacy is maintained, it is directly connected to the related questions. Thus it is often argued by some blacks that every discriminatory move by whites in the area of housing, employment, or political power and the intense opposition to intermarriage is indicative of a connectedness with race supremacy. [Therefore, the centrality of *race-place* in the transracial communicator's mind obliterates every conceivable advance in interacting with persons of another race.] When someone raises the question of housing, he views it first in terms of his *race-place* and then seeks rationalizations for what is perceived as an unethical position. To discuss housing discrimination with such a person is to touch upon the central-belief area.

It is also possible to arouse other feelings. During the height of the school busing controversy, a contingent of twenty mothers from Pontiac, Michigan, marched on Washington. One marcher had a picket sign that read "FORCED BUSING LEADS TO FORCED INTERRACIAL MARRIAGES." Whatever the other arguments for or against busing, this woman's position was clearly tied to *race-place*. We can never be successful in transracial communication if we accept the position that *race-place* is definitive in terms of our view of the world.

In communication, the beliefs representing more or less arbitrary matters of taste, with fewer functional connections, are frequently the ones changed in transracial communication. This is both fortunate and unfortunate. It is fortunate because at least beliefs are being changed, and although there is no great altering of the central beliefs, the change in periphery beliefs affects certain actions. Unfortunately, these beliefs deal merely with matters of taste, so that a person might hold conversation with a Puerto Rican at a party because he is available, but complain bitterly if the Puerto Rican moved into the neighborhood. [Arbitrary matters of taste do not affect functional connections as would central beliefs]

## STEREOTYPES

Stereotyping is a way of patterning that allows us to make shortcuts in our thinking. And because our actions are usually based upon our cognitions, stereotypes are influential in our communicative behavior. As they relate to persons of different ethnic or racial backgrounds from our own, stereotypes tend to provide us with images that we incorporate into our world, or community view. Thus, Afro-Americans are considered by others to be militant, Mexican-Americans are considered showy, and Japanese-Americans are considered humble; and whites are called vicious or conniving.[3]

Stereotyping is particularly dangerous for transracial communicators because it prejudices the communicators before they interact. If you believe all whites to be conniving before you interact with whites, then you are not likely to enter totally and honestly into communication with a white person—at least, until you are satisfied that he will not take your life or property. Similarly, a person who feels that Mexican-Americans are lazy will communicate with Mexican-Americans with that stereotype in the foreground; and one who believes that all Japanese-Americans are gardeners will interact on that basis, watching and waiting for an opportunity to spot deviations from the accepted stereotype or to verify the preconceived notion.

Perhaps the principal menace of stereotyping is that it does not allow the communicator to see the other person singly, as a unique individual. Every human being is

[3]Dennis Masaaki Ogawa, "Small Group Communication Stereotypes of Black Americans," *Journal of Black Studies*, 1, No. 3 (1971), 273–81.

unique; each of us differs from other people and possesses qualities that make us individual. Stereotyping robs a person of his individuality and obstructs transracial communicators. In fact, to be an effective participant in transracial communication demands that we respond to each other as individuals. This response is necessary even if after our interaction it is discovered that our worst fears were substantiated regarding the other person.

# LACK OF BASIC SKILLS

In one sense, all that we have been talking about in this book is a problem of communication skills; however, as it is used here, *communication skills* refers to those mechanics of producing a clear, audible message for another person. Transracial communication presents no unique difficulties in this area, although occasionally persons from one ethnic background might be accustomed to a certain kind of vocal intonation and cannot understand a person of a different background. Let me illustrate with a real-life situation.

About five years ago, a young black girl from Alabama took a commercial bus to Chicago, where she was to be met by her uncle and aunt at the bus terminal. But upon arriving in Chicago, she did not see her relatives, so she decided to take a seat in the terminal and wait. In the meantime, the uncle and aunt arrived and asked the information officer to page the girl. He did this promptly, but there was no response. She was paged a second and a third time, but did not respond. On one occasion, she asked a white man seated next to her what name was being called, and his answer confirmed her opinion that it was not her name. Finally, the uncle and aunt decided to leave the terminal, and near the exit they saw their niece on one of the benches. After a warm greeting, the aunt asked the niece why she hadn't responded to the paging. The young girl answered that it didn't *sound* like her name.

This incident might appear insignificant alone, but when you consider the hundreds of misunderstandings that occur each day because of pronunciation and patterns of intonation, then communication skills become important. These problems are sure to occur as long as people move from one place to another, but even so we must not attribute everything to a lack of communication skills. There was an absence of understanding in this case because the two systems, the announcer and the girl, had been programmed differently, to use computer terminology, as to sounds. Thus she could not understand what was being said even though she was listening—indicating that communication skills include not only the source's skills but also the listener's.

## INADEQUATE PERCEPTION

The fundamental principle of cognitive development, and hence the register of human communication, is perception. Clearly, how people interact in transracial contexts is determined by how they perceive and conceive of the other person and of reality. For, as we shall learn, perception is at the center of human judgment and interaction.

When persons are engaged in interpersonal communication, their perceptions are constantly changing. This can be attributed to the dynamism of language, which gives the perceiver reason to alter his perceptions as the conversation, speech, or discussion takes place. As it is possible for a listener to attend a public speech with a fixed attitude about the speaker and to have that attitude changed with new perceptions suggested and encouraged by the speech, so it is possible for transracial communications to change attitudes because of continuous perceptions. Several years ago, a group of militants sat listening to a Catholic priest challenge them to nonviolent action. Their initial attitudes toward the speaker and his ideas had been negative, but as the priest continued his arguments, the militants were able to accept his position. New facts and perceptions *can* change attitudes.

But perception in transracial communication is transactional. That is, source and receiver are busily developing attitudes based upon their perceptions of each other in any communication engagement. In this sense, the source is not alone in perceptual activity. The receiver is engaged in perceptual activity of his own. Whenever a white person gets communicatively involved with a black person, there are initial perceptions on both sides as the parties attempt to discover the verity or falsity of prior perceptions.

In fact, perceptions are dependent upon points of view; we often see what we want to see, or what we need to see. This can be illustrated by asking two or more people with diverse backgrounds to tell you what they see in an object; more likely than not, a farmer would see a tree differently from a naturalist. Actually, varied schools of art have grown up around artistic perception, since some artists see one thing in a bowl of fruit and others see something else. But the truth of the matter is that there is usually some validity to our perceptions, even though our view is of only one angle.

When a communicator consistently sees only one angle (and particularly if it is what he needs to see), the communication of his perceptions might indicate bias. The lack of flexibility in his perceptions frequently suggests that he had approached the situation with his mind already made up; as with a baked cake, all the ingredients had been added and nothing could be altered.

Toch and MacLean explore perception in action as a transaction, over against the idea of perception as a simple encounter with reality and the recording of impressions.[4] Their concept grows out of the earlier formulations of Dewey and Bentley, who argued that man-in-action was not over against an environing world, "but as action *of* and *by* the world in which man belongs as an integral constituent."[5] For our discussion of perception within transracial contexts, this idea is essentially sound and meaningful, inasmuch as the source and receiver are at the time being influenced and affected, even though they bring to the interaction prior perceptions. Toch and MacLean quite correctly see that perceptual communalities are established by virtue of human beings living in proximity to one another. In fact, shared meanings are central to the creation of community; the union one person feels with another when they both understand the meaning of making love, toasting a drink, and smiling

[4]Hans Toch and Malcolm S. MacLean, Jr., "Perception and Communication: A Transactional View," *Audio Visual Communication Review*, 10 (1967), 55–77.

[5]John Dewey and Arthur F. Bentley, *Knowing and the Known* (Boston: Beacon Press, 1960), p. 228.

delightfully minimizes communication problems. In interracial communication, persons engaged in conversation frequently may not understand each other because of perceptual details largely confined to one group; however, there are communalities within the American society that all may share. Furthermore, certain perceptions are accepted generally. In America, when one person smiles at another, that expression is usually understood to suggest gentleness and kindness.

Of particular interest to our discussion is the fact that within American society, as in all societies, divergences in perceptions are based upon differences of experiences. Perhaps the white person who responds negatively to the Afro-American or Mexican-American's plight is not racist but ignorant, in that his experiences have been limited. On the contrary, the deliberate racist has to possess a conception of other people that causes him to respond negatively; in truth he is usually one of the complaints. But the Iowa or Montana farmhand who has seldom seen a black person is more liable to be ignorant of the prejudices and injustices against minority persons. And in conversation, his lack of perceptions may be interpreted as racism when he may be only a most naive participant.

This is not to say that persons cannot be racist without perceiving the specific circumstances surrounding injustices. Many whites have thought they understood "our Negroes" and have developed stereotypes from split-level acquaintances with maids, gardeners, and butlers, only to find that their knowledge of blacks is extremely superficial. Put simply, racist attitudes, like ignorance, can exist anywhere. A few years ago, amid the national debate on poverty, a southern senator denied conditions of poverty within twenty-five miles of his home. He refused to believe that black people were starving and freezing to death in close proximity to where he lived. Such monumental ignorance of conditions by a U.S. senator is a concrete indication that what we see is often a consequence of our purpose, needs, and past experiences.

Occasionally, when interracial communicators proceed to interact on the assumption that their perceptions perfectly coincide, they are heading for a dead end. A person born into an environment that constantly preaches his inferiority is not likely to have the same perceptions of events and situations as a person born into an environment that suggests his superiority. Divergences in perspectives are produced by experiences, and the outlooks of minorities and whites have been divergent in America for a long time. In learning to communicate effectively, we develop our ability to perceive as nearly as possible what the other person perceives, thereby minimizing communication noise.

# seven

# *SYMBOLS*
# *IN*
# *TRANSRACIAL*
# *COMMUNICATION*

# Objectives

1.   *Define* symbol.
2.   *Discuss in writing the function of symbols in society.*
3.   *List five symbols that are monoethnic although they exist in a multiethnic community.*
4.   *Explain how symbols influence communication between people of different races.*

The fundamental premise in our analytic thrust into transracial interactions is that symbols hang societies together. Because man creates symbols, he is responsible for the effect of those symbols upon himself and his fellows. Hugh Duncan is correct in believing that how man communicates determines something about socialization.[1] But even more, man is socialized according to a continuous generation of symbols, and the results of that symbol generation bear witness to the centrality of self-image in socialization. The transference of the symbolic message must comply with certain presentational forms and restrictions. Hence, in order for a symbol to communicate to receivers, certain accepted guidelines must be followed. In fact, it can easily be argued that the closer the symbolic message conforms to the traditional expectations of the receivers, the truer the reception will be. Our reception of symbols is, as discussed earlier, dependent in part upon our ethnic perspective. Now in transference of a symbolic message to receivers, the transferer seeks to organize, arrange, and treat his symbol so as to secure the reception of the receivers. What he seeks is very often the acceptance of a symbol by those who share the same ethnic perspective. It is because of this limited conception of *symbolic structuring* that the American society has experienced a fractured socialization. All

[1]Hugh Dalziel Duncan, *Symbols in Society* (New York: Oxford University Press, Inc., 1968), pp. 21–23.

this seems monumental indeed. But what is needed is an expansion of ethnic perspectives and a reconceptualization of symbolic structuring. Let us begin this task by looking at the kinds of symbols that present us with transracial problems.

## SYMBOLS

A symbol for us means something that refers both to itself and to something other than itself because of reason, convention, or relationship. In this view, the symbol becomes basic to human society, because all things have referents. Muhammad Ali, the boxer, is a symbol of skill and power, but there is symbolic truth in the man himself. Something has to refer to the symbol, and, tautologically perhaps, the symbol suggests itself.

### Symbol Function

There are several ways to look at symbolic function. Weber contended that "in content, status honor is normally expressed by the fact that above all else a specific style of life can be expected from all those who wish to belong to the circle."[2] Status honor becomes in his view the basis of social order. Duncan expresses a similar conception of what symbols do when he says, "We march to death in the name of God ('In the sign we conquer'), country, ideology, destiny, or way of life." He believes that symbolic integration depends upon naming.[3] But this view is simply an extension of what Jahn has described as the traditional African concept of *Nommo*, the

[2] *Ibid.*
[3] *Ibid.*

**84**

generative power of words.[4] In transracial communication we use the symbols within our society, and these symbols are frequently destructive to effective interethnic interaction.

Our efforts to defend and uphold one way of thinking have led to insensitivity to the possibilities in transracial communication. Truly, there is no one set of symbols that is always correct and satisfying for all people; there are only numerous possibilities, some more fulfilling than others. To act because you feel your dignity, honor, liberty, and freedom are threatened is to move because of the functions of those terms in society. This is a kind of relationship sharing entered into by the communicators and the symbols. There need be nothing else but the saved word to send some people against others in armed conflict. Thus symbols acquire or receive sanctity and become the territory of those who view it in the same light. If we attempt, in whatever societal context we operate, to act as if our set of symbols is the only possible one, we are inevitably led into conflict with people who have an equally strong sense of symbols. But there are cases of symbolic hegemony, a sort of imposed value-symbol matrix, over a whole society.

## Symbolic Imperialism

The imposition of a single symbol system onto a multiethnic population is one way to describe the American society. In the contest between good and bad principles, correct and incorrect procedures, and socially acceptable and unacceptable practices, Western (primarily Anglo-Saxon) ideals and symbols, although they often

---

[4]Janheinz Jahn, *Muntu: An Outline of Neo-African Culture* (New York: Grove Press, Inc., 1961), pp. 125–32.

struggled among themselves, succeeded in a symbolic imperialism of the first order. While in some societies the symbols of the indigenous and enslaved peoples became accepted into the society, in America neither the indigenous nor the enslaved peoples' values figured in the creation of a symbol system. What occurred in American society was the development of a symbol system that enshrined European symbols on foreign soil.

Is it possible to discover the fundamental premise upon which this symbolic imperialism is based? One premise might involve the whole question of the superiority or the inferiority of races. The European belief in the white race's superiority is centuries old. This, coupled with the early Americans' notion of a "favored people," produced a race unable to accept ideals contrary to their world view. Racism, then, is initially established within the structure of society. In such a society, images, concepts, and symbols had to reflect the likeness of their creators, who were, at that moment in history, incapable of the necessary generosity to conceive a system based upon a multiethnic reality. They produced a society designed for Europeans but comprised of various other races.

## Principal Symbols

An exploration of *symbolic structuring*, the *creation* of things to suggest other things by relationship and convention, will reveal the difficulty of transracial communication in a society predicated on a single ethnic perspective. To begin with, a certain invisibility of other peoples to the eyes of whites has meant that whites talk to each other about their values and symbols. Consequently, some blacks have started to respond as if whites were invisible, often leaving whites with a sense of helplessness. Obviously this is an excellent lesson in the effects on others of talking only to people who are like yourself. But in the end it is not enough. From this point we must begin to build *symbolic pluralism*, the structuring of which requires conviction and skill.

Among the principal symbols of the society that have fostered the hegemony of white images is the Constitution. Although it is a document of considerable insight, it is a white document that was written for whites. And the endeavor to make it work for a multiethnic nation has caused extreme frustration. For a homogeneous nation it seemed perfect; but America was not homogeneous, and the conflicts and difficulties in human interaction may be the results of an inadequate symbol system. That the Constitution is a white document with more meaning for whites has been only one aspect of the problem. Indeed, it is possible for symbols of one ethnic group to be universal. But this is not possible when the internal composition of the symbol is antithetical to other groups or when the symbol is forced upon different peoples. We need symbols that will underscore a multiethnic society and help to create a favorable transracial environment. The question is one of perspective upon facts—indeed, upon experiences. How symbols come to be monoethnically representational is of chief concern.

When the "Founding Fathers" (which, of course, is a monoethnic representation) came together to draw up the Constitution, their perception was of a white nation governing itself. Exclusivity was built in definitionally as they hammered out upon the anvil of society such problems as the nature of representation in the Congress and the census of the southern states whose numbers were enlarged by the Africans within their midst. Furthermore, the failure to set an immediate date for the end of the slave trade and slavery was indicative of a "white" rather than a "multiethnic" national conceptualization. It is this initial base that has influenced how we, in this society, interact across racial lines.

Because the mass of whites in our society have selected the symbols that allow them to maintain or achieve order in their associations with each other, ethnic minorities, Appalachian hillbillies, and Louisiana Cajuns have seldom been included in the total symbol system. But blacks (Afro-Americans), chicanos (Mexican-Americans), and native Americans (Indians) have been the least integrated into the system. Starting from a racial base, the mass of whites who have seen phenomena only from an ethnocentric vantage point seem incapable of dealing with symbolic pluralism.

Santa Claus is one example of a Western symbol that fails to consider the diversity of American society. Few thinking black parents could accept this symbol for their children because they, as the gift bringers, cannot share in the ethnicity of the Santa Claus image. As a representative Western symbol of giving, Santa Claus is adequate, but for blacks and some other ethnic or religious groups, he is inadequate. Thus, Jews in California have begun a Hanu-Claus (from *Hanukkah*) and blacks in Chicago a Saint Soul. This method of symbol structuring, however, does not answer the fundamental problem. What occurs is a substitution of name and, perhaps, uniform, but the symbols remain exclusive. This might be considered healthy, inasmuch as it represents a first step away from the hegemony of a white Western Santa Claus over every ethnic group, but it is far from adequate. Neither Saint

Soul nor Hanu-Claus can claim universality; and if they did, it would be a repetition of the white Santa Claus. Saint Soul's role is not universal, as Santa Claus' is not; they are both ethnic manifestations. It is nonsense in human communication to assume that because of its ethnic identity, one symbol is superior to the other and should be universally accepted because of that identity.

Let us now consider additional symbols to demonstrate our point. As the Constitution and Santa Claus are reflections of white unconscious racist behavior, the deliberate construction of a statue, or the assembling of "great men of the twentieth century" on the windows of a church, points to a white orientation in the making of relationships.

An artist was commissioned to design a statue, the "Spirit of Detroit," for placement in the Detroit civic center—an innocent enough, and perhaps noble, aspiration. As a man of the people, he created an image of a white Anglo-Saxon. Nearly one million blacks live in Detroit, and they can find no civic pride or relationship in what was supposed to be "the Spirit of Detroit." A pragmatic test of symbolic representativeness is the question, What would other people create if they could wield the power? Most assuredly, blacks would not create a "Spirit of Detroit" with absolutely Anglo-Saxon features. But were whites as invisible to blacks as blacks seem to whites, an Afro-coiffured statue might appear. Such talk, however, is meaningless, inasmuch as most blacks are actively engaged in contact and associations with whites by necessity; on the other hand, whites generally tend to associate with blacks by choice. Knowledge of and sensitivity to white values is probably stronger among blacks than in the reverse situation.

A more serious problem than the creation of the unrepresentative symbol is the climate that fostered the growth of such exclusivity. To say that racism has penetrated every fabric of our society is an admission of the magnitude of the problem. What gives rise to the invention of racist symbols, however innocent? And still further, how can creators constantly fail to be representative? These are tough questions, but so is the problem addressed by them. The one million black people of Detroit were not considered when the "Spirit of Detroit" was erected, because the society has habitually operated without reference to any minority groups. To say the least, transracial communicators must begin on even this elemental level to develop symbols with common appeal across ethnic lines. One can begin to do this on a one-to-one basis without waiting for some miracle; the manual of communication is that the miracle is within you as a person. As you communicate with your friends, of similar or different ethnic backgrounds, practice referring to symbols that appeal across ethnic lines. You might warm up to this difficult task by thinking of some symbols that are amenable to another view.

Another example of a white Western symbolic structuring bias was the announcement by Grace Episcopal Cathedral Church in San Francisco that ten men had been selected to have their faces appear on church windows as the "greatest men of the twentieth century." Needless to say, not one of them was other than white. Such gross ethnocentrism is both self-deceiving to the creators and abhorrent to thinking people. In some cases, omission of relevant data is deliberate; perhaps in most, it is a function of insensitivity to other people. I remember inquiring of a colleague as to why his new textbook did not make use of one black literary figure when he had used hundreds of whites. His reply, sorrowful enough, was that it had never crossed his mind during the writing of the book. Such lack of sensitivity, while not usually malicious, has the same effect, because the organizers and opinion makers of society control to a large extent how we relate, and effective communication between persons of different races is interaction informed by the use of meaningful symbols.

It is striking, in fact, that the possibilities of demonstrating communicative efficacy between members of different races has hardly been explored. Relevant to such a demonstration would be the application of certain theoretical concepts outlined above. For instance, the transracial communicator must be capable of understanding the basis of symbols employed in society, and of utilizing his knowledge of facts and experience of phenomena to broaden the basis of those symbols to accommodate other ethnic perspectives. The expression, "as disciplined as the Spartans," might become, in the mind of a transracial communicator, "as disciplined as the Zulu," or, "as disciplined as the Apache." You see, each ethnic group could probably illustrate that its people were the most disciplined warriors in history. And while there is certainly nothing wrong with the Spartan example, the communicator who is ignorant of its ethnocentric base will most definitely have problems. The following discussion on symbolic racism further explicates, by examples, the pervasiveness of symbolic imperialism.

## SYMBOLS AND RACISM

We have discussed the need for symbolic structuring as we explained the analytic thrust into interracial interactions. Now we shall explore a kind of racism imposed by symbols upon a multiethnic society by specific references to images and concepts. Of necessity, this discussion will indicate the fallacies inherent in monoethnic symbols when applied to a multiracial society. Alternatives for transracial understanding will be presented in an effort to point the reader toward resolution of conflict.

Symbols are found in all societies. As common points of reference, they help human beings to make judgments, assess decisions, organize ideals, and speak knowledgeably. However, as will be demonstrated, symbols can also be detrimental to the spirit of unity in a multiracial society. Those symbols that affirm the self-concepts of one group, encouraging ethnocentricity and race narcissism, are frequently adverse to other groups. The following examples tend to reflect symbolic racism in our society.

## Monoethnicity in the Flesh and the Nude

What is flesh-colored? And what is the nude look? We assume, of course, in asking these questions, that the person who speaks of the nude look has something more in mind than a naked body. In a multiethnic and multiracial context with people of African, Asian, and European descent, it is rather nonsensical to talk of flesh-colored cosmetics, clothing, or bandages. Those manufacturers who find it necessary to have "flesh-colored" products might contribute to transracial harmony by having many different shades, as is the case with women's hosiery. In general, until recently the cosmetics manufacturers developed their products exclusively for whites, and Oriental, Mexican-American, or Afro-American women had to do the best they could with white products. Needless to say, such makeshift and "make do" was not alto-gether successful or satisfactory.

In addition, the "nude look" was developed as a white appeal; a curvaceous black model was not in the mind of the manufacturers. For a multiethnic society, the "nude look" might utilize several shades of skin, and thus not impose white concepts imperialistically upon other peo-ple. This is definitely what has happened in the area of eye makeup, where Orientals are completely forgotten. Despite the growing number of Americans of Asian an-cestry, manufacturers still design eye makeup almost ex-clusively for women with "double" eyelids. Most Oriental women have "single" eyelids; they do not have ridges across their eyelids, so essential to some European beauty standards. Instead, Oriental women have an epicanthic fold that creates a slanted-eye look. Because of the im-position of occidental standards upon the society, some Oriental girls desire to have the extra layer of fat removed from their eyelids so that they may look more Caucasian. The sustaining of monoethnic symbolism depends upon the awareness of the community to the reality of the soci-ety, and manufacturers might do several things to alle-viate this area of disharmony. For example, the produc-tion of a line of products for Oriental women might aid in creating a favorable image of single eyelids. When we foster industries that do not have a multiracial sensitivity, we encourage disharmony that will surely plague our transracial interactions.

To talk, in the sense of conversation, with a person of another culture without the awareness of these prob-lem areas is to tread onto unsafe territory unless you are a most astute conversationalist. The college president at a major university received a delegation of chicano students. He listened thoroughly to their complaints, and at the end of their session, said enthusiastically, "I appreciate your concern for a relevant education. I've just asked the dean to search for a Black Studies director." Well, you can guess the reactions of these Mexican-American students now that the president had made an embarrassing mistake by not even recognizing their own unique demand for curriculum relevance. After all, chicanos represent the largest minority group in the Southwest. The manufacturers who continue to develop and advertise "flesh-colored" products are just as insensitive to a multiracial society as the college president appeared to be.

## Standards of Beauty: Tall, Thin, and Dark

Transracial communication is concerned with extending consciousness in those areas where we are not knowledgeable. The concepts and ideas of beauty as promulgated by such contests as "Miss America" are representatively white in their orientation. Because of the "beauty contests" that have become big commercial business, it is extremely difficult to combat the ethnocentric ideas of beauty in a multiracial society. The essence of American womanhood is not necessarily conveyed in the symbolic use of the contest. Perhaps some of the contests should follow the lead of the "Miss Black America" pageants in order to be more realistic. A "Miss White America" contest would highlight the ethnic standards involved, and there would be little reason for an Oriental or Afro-American girl to expect admission. On the other hand, the elimination of the hypocrisy by reorganizing and restructuring the show might be beneficial. The essential qualities of womanhood are not the sole possessions of one race or ethnic group. At the University of Hawaii, located in multiracial Honolulu, eight queens are chosen, from each of several racial groups, to reign over festivities. Along with the imposed white standards of beauty on the whole society has come the emphasis on blondness. For whites, blondness has a unique attraction, so much so that whites have adages relating to it. Thus, "Blondes have more fun" and "Gentlemen prefer blondes" indicate the esteem blondness holds for white Americans. But such admiration is not necessarily characteristic or typical of other Americans. Symbolic racism is manifest when this symbol is presented with no attention to cultural diversity.

Another indication of the white American's disregard of other races within the society is the slogan, "tall, dark, and handsome," which usually carries a reference to the physical appearance of white men. The paradox is that darkness is perceived as a symbol of male attractiveness to white women. However, it can be rather confusing, because a black man might be tall and handsome, yet whites would probably not describe him as "tall, dark, and handsome." This is further complicated because black men come in various shades of darkness. But the essence of such a slogan is found in its underlying assumptions. The first assumption is that the society is composed of whites, and thus, "tall, dark, and handsome" can only refer to one group. Another assumption is that it is impossible for white women to consider black men attractive; so "dark" really means a white man who is darker than other white men. In transracial communication, a person understanding this contradiction might expand the consciousness of another by responding to the slogan with the alternative "tall, white, but darker than the average white, and handsome." In this way the paradox is exposed.

## Authority Images

In a recent move to update the U.S. Army's image and make it more attractive to youth, the public relations people began changing the famous poster with the face of an old, bearded man pointing his index finger and saying, "I want you," to a more egalitarian and youthful poster picturing several smiling young men and captioned, "The army wants to join you." While this shift in public relations indicates that the army has given some thought to communicating with youth, it fails to demonstrate that the army recognizes the ethnic and racial diversity within the target population. Despite the new posters, blacks who could never feel identification with the picture of an old white man saying "I want you" have little more identification with the new one. The argument for symbolic engineering takes on significant meaning when one understands that inadequately directed symbols lead to misunderstanding and frustration.

Perhaps just as extensive within the society is the symbol of Jesus Christ represented in pictures as white. Transracial communication is impeded when the symbols around which we hold conversation are inherently racist in nature. Such a situation retards normalization of the communication process because it distorts reality for a multiethnic society. Archie Bunker, of the popular CBS television series "All in the Family," would probably say, "You mean to tell me Jesus wasn't white?" Of course, the difficulty lies not in the conception but in the perception, inasmuch as the idea is perfectly legitimate, but the discernment, which emerges as the picture of a white man with long hair, is clearly poorly focused for a multi-ethnic society. Maulana Karenga, a leading figure in the black nationalist movement in the decade of the sixties was fond of saying, "Black who prays to someone who looks like George Wallace with long hair got a lots to be scared of." What he was expressing was the symbolic unrepresentativeness of the popular image of Jesus as it was presented in common paintings and pictures. In fact, awareness of this symbolic inadequacy led to the establishment of the Shrine of the Black Madonna in Detroit, Michigan, a few years ago. While there exists an argument for symbols based in the people's ethnicity that are not psychologically hazardous, the dominance of any ethnic symbolism must be discouraged when it is imposed on other groups as a standard. Transracial communicators must be concerned with altering the preexisting adaptations to the environment, because in so doing they assert the primacy of transraciality and signal the normalization of communication between differing and different people.

Symbolic racism circumscribes our communication. What is left for persons of different ethnic or racial backgrounds to discuss is more limited than it would otherwise be if the symbols within the environment were multiethnic. The alternatives to this situation are chiefly found in responses that open new symbolic paths in an effort to restructure the existing patterns of communication.

# eight

# DETERMINANTS

# OF

# NORMALIZATION

# Objectives

AFTER READING THIS CHAPTER, YOU SHOULD BE ABLE TO:

1.  List J. L. Austin's three types of speech acts.
2.  Discuss in writing how illocutionary speech acts are related to transracial communication.
3.  Describe metacommunication.
4.  Discuss how the "subtle agenda" can influence transracial communication.
5.  List three instances of the "subtle agenda" from your experiences.
6.  Describe how sex and racism relate to transracial communication.
7.  Explain what is meant by intervening symbol.
8.  Describe how perception and purpose operate in transracial communication between persons of opposite sexes.
9.  Explain vertical hierarchy.
10.  Explain how negative perception can influence transracial communication.
11.  Demonstrate the symbolic reverse.
12.  Distinguish between trust and credibility.
13.  Give in writing some examples of routinization of communication.
14.  Write an essay explaining why transracial communication is important.

# SPEECH ACTS IN TRANSRACIAL CONTEXTS

J. L. Austin defined three types of speech acts—that is, acts that are performed when language is used: locutionary, illocutionary, and perlocutionary acts.[1] Simply put, a locutionary act is the speaker's act of saying something; an illocutionary act is one the speaker performs *in* saying whatever it is he says; and a perlocutionary act is one the speaker performs *by* saying something.

According to Austin, we cannot determine the illocutionary act that is performed until we know how the locution is being used. He lists several examples:

Asking or answering a question
Giving some information or an assurance or a warning
Announcing a verdict or an intention
Pronouncing a sentence
Making an appointment or an appeal or criticism
Making an identification or giving a description[2]

Illocutionary acts must be distinguished from perlocutionary acts intending to produce effects upon the feelings, thoughts, or actions of the listeners.

For the person interested in transracial communication, the category of illocutionary acts is extremely signifi-

[1] J. L. Austin, *How to Do Things with Words* (New York: Oxford University Press, 1962), p. 98.
[2] *Ibid.*

cant as a mirror of the fundamental difficulties that are experienced between persons of different races. While perlocutions are also important and are a real part of our daily interactions, it is in the more subtle area of illocutions that most of our misunderstandings and conflicts arise. Thus, it is to our advantage to examine this category carefully.

When persons of two or more races come together in verbal interaction, they may readily employ illocutionary acts. Locutions (the act of saying whatever you say) have a way of turning into "illocutionary forces" very rapidly, so that a person might begin with asking a question or pronouncing a judgment or a sentence before he knows it. Although illocutionary acts can be positive and contributive to good communication, the wrong choices can establish moods, directions, and reactions that will hinder interracial relations through speech. The person who gets the impression that another person announces, demands, or argues before he knows his listener may give second thoughts to transracial communication. Therefore, what you do with words—that is, *in* saying and *by* saying what you say—is critically important to the sensitive person. We all want to feel that we are sovereign, with some right to evaluate, listen, and interact without some person spouting illocutions.

Normalization of the communicative situation can be effected only by our careful anticipation of illocutionary speech acts, and the understanding that they may impede communication transracially. Because the primary difficulty of transracial communication is the concept of race itself, most, if not all, illocutionary speech acts have implications for transracial interactions.

# METACOMMUNICATION

In transracial communication, human beings transmit more than the words that make up language. Metacommunication indicates to the persons involved in verbal interaction what type of responses should be made to the communication. It is the nonverbal cues, gestures, or other physical expressions given by the speaker, or it is the vocal tone, pitch, or inflection.

Because transracial communication inherently must consider the differences of people, it is often constrained by such metacommunication cues as skin color, texture of hair, and general physical appearance. Additionally, the person's dialect might be a metacommunication cue, inasmuch as people frequently listen as much to *how* you say as to *what* you say. Several whites have demonstrated, by chemically changing the color of their skin, that whites in America generally react negatively to darker skin colors before they hear discussion or conversation relating to issues.

If our reactions to others are influenced by factors other than the content of their messages, we are the subjects of metacommunication. Actually this means that all our communication is influenced by some metacommunication because we never respond to words in isolation. Even the most precise language that can be shared between people is subject to the innuendoes of vocal inflection, facial expressions, and physical appearance. For blacks to respond to whites in transracial communication or vice versa with any fidelity means that the communicators must not allow metacommunication cues to prohibit effective interaction. This does not mean that communicators can avoid the effects of metacommunication, but rather that those effects will not be the sole inputs into their interaction.

The nature of metacommunication cues can frequently be disconcerting and confusing. The ethnic-minority person who reacts with observable agreement—nods, smiles, etc.—during a talk with a person of the white ethnic majority may simultaneously be wishing curses upon the white person. Thus what we see—indeed, what we hear—is not always what the sender's real message is. The girl who says "no" while responding to her lover's caresses is not too convincing; metacommunication cues affirm what verbal cues seem to deny.

## The Subtle Agenda

By "subtle agenda," we mean the idiosyncratic physical behaviors that an individual brings with him in interpersonal communication. It is subtle because frequently the individual communicator does not know that it exists and can jeopardize transracial communication without his knowledge. For instance, when the white teacher of an elementary school was approached by two students, one white and one black, she was noticed to lean toward the white child, keeping the hand nearest to him free, but shifting her weight away from the black child and picking up the class roll book with the hand nearest the black pupil. The message may be unintentional but the impact on the child who was slighted is unmistakable. Metacommunication cues are the mirrors to our innermost feelings when they are reflected in physical movement. It is not always so easy to get at those "subtle agendas" that are a part of our physical makeup. Because each individual is a composite of physical movement, no two persons will always have the same physical behavior. Misunderstanding can occur, however, when these movements convey negative attitudes about the person with whom we are trying to communicate.

Subtle agendas are not necessarily negative; but when they are, they contribute to hard feelings and suspicions. Several blacks have sworn that they can walk into a room with whites and identify those who are biased against blacks. Most of what these individuals have to go on is metacommunication. It might be as slight as the glint in the eye or the twitch of the nose. You really do not have to say anything to be heard and understood.

## SEX AND TRANSRACIAL COMMUNICATION

As early as Knower[3] and as recently as Furbay,[4] the evidence demonstrates that women are more persuasible than men. In addition, Exline, Gray, and Schuette[5] found that women were more likely to engage in mutual visual interactions when paired with persons of the opposite sex. However, these studies, and many like them, lack the dimension of race. On the basis of present studies,

[3]Franklin Knower, "Experimental Studies in Changes of Attitudes: A Study of the Effects of Printed Arguments on Changes of Attitudes," *Journal of Abnormal and Social Psychology*, 30 (1936), 522–32.

[4]Albert Furbay, "The Influence of Scattered Versus Compact Seating on Audience Response," *Speech Monographs*, 32 (1965), 144–48.

[5]Ralph Exline, David Gray, and Dorothy Schuette, "Visual Behavior in a Dyad as Affected by Interview Content and Sex of Respondent," *Journal of Personality and Social Psychology*, 1 (1965), 201–9.

**105**

we know that white women are more persuasible than white men, but we do not know if the variable of race would significantly alter the results. Are white women more persuasible if a message is transmitted by a black, brown, or white male? There are numerous possibilities for investigation in similar questions. As it stands, we also know that white females engage in mutual visual interaction more readily than white males, but we do not know whether black females respond similarly. Thus, this section will explore race and sex in communication in an effort to generate and elucidate hypotheses for experimental researchers.

## Intervening Symbolism

We shall explore several aspects of race and sex, dealing first with the intervening symbolism of white women, and then describing the various manifestations of superficial interaction between whites and all minority racial and ethnic groups because of the intervening symbolism. The term *intervening symbol* for "white womanhood" is used as an analog for the presence of racism in America. In this sense, it is not the white woman who fractures American society, but the symbol created to protect her virtue. Thus Asian-Americans and Mexican-Americans who have never lived in the South in great numbers are as affected by this symbol as Afro-Americans. In fact, whites, males and females, are the most abject victims. In the past, elaborate legal systems were frequently established to prevent interracial contacts of a sexual nature, but they also succeeded in making *any* communication between black men and white women suspect.[6] And any conversation between white men and

[6]See Calvin Hernton, *Sex and Racism in America* (New York: Grove Press, Inc., 1965), *passim.*

black women was also reason for question. People seemed to ask, What have they got to talk about? And in the case of the black male and white female, it meant that conversations could never be genuine. Each party had to protect his or her statements lest the whites of the community angrily disapprove. For the white male and the black female, the conversation had to be equally empty. Little that was genuine could be said when the parties viewed each other as objects and not real human beings. Perfunctory talk, much like the greeting, has always occurred between blacks and whites in the South, but seldom have people really talked. Standing squarely in the center of any interracial conversation was always the specter of the intervening symbol. Lillian Smith writes:

> The more trails the white man made to backyard cabins, the higher he raised his white wife on her pedestal when he returned to the big house. The higher the pedestal, the less he enjoyed her whom he had put there, for statues after all are only nice things to look at.[7]

Symbols determine how people interact. The intervening symbol meant that blacks had always to interact with whites on terms that were set by those who created the sacred mythology. W. J. Cash writes, in *The Mind of the South*:

> She was the South's Palladium, the southern woman— shield-bearing Athena gleaming whitely in the clouds, the standard for its rallying, the mystic symbol of its nationality in face of the foe. She was the lily-pure maid of Astolat and the hunting goddess of the Boeotian hill. And—she was the pitiful Mother of God. Merely to mention her was to send strong men into tears—or shouts. There was

[7]Lillian Smith, *Killers of the Dream* (New York: Doubleday & Company, Inc., 1963), p. 103.

hardly a sermon that did not begin and end with tributes in her honor, hardly a brave speech that did not open and close with clashing of shields and flourishing of swords for her glory.[8]

Thus, lurking behind every sentence, every word, spoken between persons of different races in the South was the intervening symbol. A black man could not ask a white woman her name, and a white man, for his name's sake, could not be seen engaging in conversation with a black woman. What occurred after dark is impossible to analyze in detail, but it is clear that the symbol of the white woman was responsible, at least in part, for the lack of normalization of interracial communication.

But what originated in the South must not be considered purely regional, because the nation generally partook of the South's ideas. And despite the changes that have been brought about because of pressures exerted by civil rights groups, the changes in attitudes have come slowly. We are able to communicate more genuinely now than at any period in the history of American society. Shuffles are out of style for everyone. But even so, we still have not eliminated every vestige of white-supremacy mythology.

Because of the symbol, the process of normalization is extremely difficult in some cases, particularly where either blacks or whites are accustomed to thinking in patterns influenced by the ideology of the lily-pure maid. All conversation takes place before the backdrop of the ideology in such instances so that communication is superficial at best and impossible at worst. Vestiges of

[8]W. J. Cash, *The Mind of the South* (New York: Vintage Books, 1960), p. 89.

this perfunctory talk are found just about everywhere and have infected every interracial interaction. Perhaps the white woman herself is most affected by this distorted symbolism that has made her involved interactions with males of different races clearly suspect.

How can we normalize the apparently abnormal communication between males and females of different races? There is not much research to inform the judgment, and therefore our answer will have to be speculative. However, speculation grounded in the practical extensions of communication research, while not science, is educational. And all positive relations between members of different races or ethnic groups are dependent upon clear communicative processes. Like all human interactions, those processes are most successful when people have a mutual respect for each other.

Communication, we know, can exist only when a message has been encoded by a source and transmitted to a receiver who decodes it. This process is essential in any type of communication situation, regardless of the sex or race of the source and receiver. Thus one answer is that we can normalize the relationship between communicators by refining the process by which the message is transmitted. Another answer, growing out of the same principle, is that the communication can be normalized by reinterpreting the images of source and receiver.

In the first instance, we attempt to remove the causes of distortion derived from the method of transmission. Communicators who recognize the significance of language in transracial interactions will have little problem with this aspect of normalization. Realization is the initial step toward understanding and communication. But realization is on the road, it is not the destination. Therefore, the communicator hoping to have effective interaction with a person of the opposite sex and another race will have to keep two things in mind: (1) purpose, and (2) perception.

What is the purpose of the communication? This cannot be fuzzy; it has to be sharp and precise. Furthermore, the receiver should have a clear understanding of the purpose, even if it is as vague as posing a threat. Between the sexes of different races, this is probably more critical than at any other time in communication, because of the compounding factors brought on by the language of courtship and romance. After all, it is frequently impossible for a woman to tell whether a man is speaking representationally or instrumentally when he says, "You have the most beautiful brown eyes in the world." If the words are meant only as a matter of fact, that is one thing. If, however, the words are used instrumentally, they are a means to another end, which might be a proposition.

Because of these factors of language, the communicators must know the purposes of their messages. This is not to say that one's purpose cannot grow out of the conversation; but even then, it should be clear and precise.

Perception is the crayon that colors the communicator's response and reaction to the world. For example, one's image of the opposite sex can affect his or her reactions. The extent to which the communication process is affected by this factor is a measure of the distortion inherent within that particular configuration. Additionally, how the one views the other sexually and racially can determine the nature of the communication. If black women are viewed stereotypically as "delightfully feminine" by persons of different races and the opposite sex, it affects the nature of the communication event. Such a manifestation of perception affecting communication appears in the numerous instances of white males speaking to black women in the South as if the woman is a prostitute. Whites' perception of the black woman as sexy and earthy has led to many instances of disrespect.

The proper perception of another communicator is one informed by affective behavior: the acceptance and respect of all people as human beings. Thus perception is an organizing concept. It is the process by which a person selects, organizes, and interprets sense stimulation into meaningful and usable patterns. In this way, the transracial communicator relates himself to other persons. In communication between the sexes of different races, perception may dictate whether interaction is normalized or not.

## SOCIAL STRATIFICATION AND TRANSRACIAL INTERACTION

Several writers have alluded to, and others have explored, the concept of social stratification within American society. In critical ways, they have argued, stratification affects our interpersonal interaction. Communication, therefore, does not escape the influence of the stratification of society. Of course, the manifestations of structure are seen in sexism and classism as well as racism.

### Vertical Hierarchy

Generally speaking, this society accords a greater place to the male person than to the female. Thus we presume, when we see a man and a woman together, that the man is the leader, expert, teacher, breadwinner, etc. There is a built-in stratification system, and so we expect the man to play the dominant role in any interaction between the sexes.

A similar argument has been made regarding the wealthy and the poor. Those who have looked for economic determinants of history have constantly reminded us that in our society, a wealthy person is presumed to have the dominant role in any interaction with a poor person. Shortly after the Attica tragedy, much conjecture was made regarding Governor Nelson Rockefeller's order of troops to storm the barricades while 38 guard-hostages were being held by the prisoners. An indicting question raised by one civilian negotiator who had talked with the prisoners is, Would the governor have ordered the troops to take the prison at all costs if 38 millionaires or 38 governors, rather than guards, had been held? The contention is that social stratification figures in most human-interaction situations.

However, vertical hierarchy in the context of trans-racial interaction may be exacerbated by class and sex perceptions. Yet the essential variable is social stratification based upon race. And a society that adopts the assumptions built into a two-category social order must mobilize forces to maintain the "status gap" between the two orders.[9]

When the factor of race is present within a communication situation—that is, where you have sources and receivers of messages—stratification may be presumed. In a study conducted by several research associates at the UCLA Center for Afro-American Studies, it

[9]Michael Banton, *Race Relations* (New York: Basic Books, Inc., Publishers, 1967), pp. 1–10.

was found that presumption of hierarchy is prevalent among whites and blacks. Furthermore, the results revealed that when whites and blacks were shown photographs of transracial interactions, they usually accorded the white person higher status. For example, when the white respondents were given a picture of two males, one white and the other black, and then asked to identify the student and the professor, almost 73 percent identified the white male as the professor. While only 52 percent of the black respondents selected the white in the highest status position, clearly the pattern of stratification exists. The person who enters transracial communication unaware of the pitfalls of "stratification thinking" is apt to participate in an empty exercise. The best way to avoid holding meaningless interactions with people of other races and ethnic groups is to be aware of affectation and to suspect stratification even if it is not readily manifest.

## Superficial Stratification

There is the perennial story of the bank president who slaps the chicano parking-lot attendant on the back, "Hi, Carlos." Carlos responds in a similar manner by slapping the president on the back and saying, "Pretty well, Johnnie, old buddy." The president's reaction to the reply is usually one of consternation. Not in his most unguarded moments could he conceive of a Mexican-American slapping him on the back and calling him by his first name. And a parking-lot attendant, at that! In a multiethnic society, the person who is defined as low-status always suspects stratification. The difficulty, however, in transracial communication is that the high-status person does not suspect stratification, not even in his own behavior. In fact, there appears to be an acceptance that things are correct and proper as they are. Such a philosophical position attracts violent reactions. The communicator must be certain that the strength of his ideas or the force of his message is not dependent upon superficial boundaries. The professor who asks for acceptance of his ideas because he is a professor, and the general who seeks adherence to his commands because of his position, are both, it is hoped, becoming relics of the past. The transracial communicator who depends upon a superficial racial hierarchy to convey his message will find little to communicate.

## Influence of Negative Perception

David K. Berlo has written that a source's attitude toward the other person in the process affects the source's behavior.[10] Let us suppose that one person is a racist who dislikes the other person's race. Now, this negative attitude is sure to cause the message to be affected, but more, it is frequently the cause for total collapse of understanding in a communication situation. This occurs when the primary receiver in the communication process perceives that the other person is a racist. Then the response of the receiver is likely to be affected, either in a hostile or reserved manner.

When our perception tells us that someone is not like us, we frequently interpret it as a negative fact. As men seek to create gods in their own image, so they do with other men. If Reynaldo thinks that H.V. or Greg does not have *machismo*, or if H.V. thinks neither Rey-

[10]David K. Berlo, *The Process of Communication* (New York: Holt, Rinehart & Winston, Inc., 1960), p. 47.

naldo nor Greg has soul, there are apt to be negative reactions. Each person's initial reaction is to measure the other person by attitudes, values, and behaviors present within himself. The closer the person we are trying to communicate with comes to our own view of ourselves, the easier it is to have meaningful interaction. Knowing this, some communicators deliberately seek to become all things to all men. They desire to be seen as their listeners see themselves. Such planned identification can lead to a restrained communicative interaction with the receivers of a message, if the receivers consider the attempted identification to be either mockery or demagoguery.

A few years ago, a popular component to speech communication theory was that of speaker–audience analysis and adaptation, emphasis and adaptation. Emphasis on a pragmatic application of Burkean concepts, rather than, say, the acceptance of Burke's ideas as explicative, has led to a belief that in every communication situation, the communicatiors must seek to merge their actions and behaviors. What is more important is what we have called *shared meanings.*

There is a tendency for shared meanings to grow out of common interests without our having to affect behavior. This attitude must be abandoned in transracial communication. Persons engaged in communicating across racial lines must recognize that each comes from a different background and cultural experience, and as a result their behaviors will not be the same and should not be affected to mock behavioral similarity. Whites have often felt they could achieve a greater degree of acceptance, for instance, among blacks by resorting to urban black language behavior—only to find that they were rejected.

Rejection does not come because of the use of the language, but because of the unreality of its use. There are clearly some whites, who have been reared with blacks, who know the idiosyncrasies of the language and can speak to "a cat making it on the streets" and be accepted by blacks, even if it causes wonderment. So the use of the language is not the difficulty, it is the imprecise use of the language to gain a result. Affectation for the cause of persuasion is taboo in transracial communication. The receiver is perceiver, and what he perceives greatly influences his response. Thus an Afro-American who would approach a native American with the statement, "Hello, heap big Indian chief," would have seriously impaired his ability to communicate. Affectation is not flattering.

One of the communicators in a transracial setting can easily feel that he is being placed in an inferior role by the apparently condescending language used by the other. Thus, vertical hierarchies are frequently set up through the use of affective behavior by the person playing the condescending role. In effect, this communicator says, "I am big enough to come down to your level, listen to me, watch me."

## Horizontal Stratification

In groups where minorities share the same or similar roles with whites, stratification is often horizontal and affects the attitude of communicators inside or outside the group. A good example is the elementary classroom, where teachers may accord status to children on the basis of race or ethnic origin. This stratification traverses class backgrounds, as the teacher still accords the upper-class black child power status, or asks him to talk to the class about poverty, or about the urban ghetto, although the child has never seen one. Assumption, then, of inferiority and superiority becomes a code of conduct for the classroom.

Stereotyping makes life simpler perhaps, but it does not make it any happier. We soon become victims of the elaborate classification schemes we create to make life simpler, and then our problems multiply. An English-speaking teacher can frequently make errors of communication in relation to Puerto Rican or Mexican-American students, based on lack of understanding of Spanish. A friend of mine tells the story of several Mexican-American students being classified as Educable Mental Retardates (EMR) because the teacher could not get them to respond. It turned out that each morning when she called the roll she would say, Joo-an Garcia, Joe-say Martinez, etc. The students thought their names were being called but did not answer because they did not want to appear dumb. Had the teacher wanted to establish a good relationship with the children, she might have asked them their names before attempting to pronounce them.

But horizontal stratification is not limited to the schools; it is found in most places where people of several ethnic backgrounds or races congregate or work. Because of its wide dispersal in most sectors of society, each individual must assume a responsibility for eliminating its racial basis, and thus its presence in transracial interactions. Normalization in transracial communication is more likely to occur when we have defined our distaste for stratification by race. One important technique for handling the initial process of stratification as it occurs in communication is the *symbolic reverse*. The *symbolic reverse* allows the alert communicator to switch the referent in a conversation. In one episode of the award-winning series, "All in the Family," two black burglars enter Archie's house; they are surprised that the white folks have a big color television setting in the living room, and they notice that "all white people's houses got the same old smell." On a more interpersonal level, an example that comes to mind is that of a young chicano boy when a black college student asked him to name the greatest American hero of the last hundred years. The boy named Emiliano Zapata. In his way he had used the symbolic reverse, although the black student had not expressed a preference for heroes. Given the chance, one young chicano boy made certain that the person would not be a United States hero.

Symbolic reverses should be used as instructional techniques, but they will also expand the consciousness of the communicators. When someone says Sammy Davis, Jr., is the black Frank Sinatra, one might respond that Frank Sinatra is the white Sammy Davis, Jr., as an instrument to make others aware of their ethnocentric statements. The symbolic reverse is an important technique in normalization.

## Power In Transracial Communication

Because each person is defined only in relationship to others and has satisfaction only when expressed in human interaction, the exercise of power or the knowledge of one's ability to exercise power determines the outcome of interpersonal communication. [Communication between whites and minority-group members suggests that power is often a key variable within a transracial context. Conceptually, power may be defined as the ability to control and determine one's own and another's social behavior. In the past, the structure of American society has dictated power relations between blacks and whites, either by custom or law. Thus, any communication of a black person with a white person had to be viewed in the light of limitations imposed upon their verbal interaction. Hence a black man in southern society, regardless of age or position with the black community, addressed a white teen-ager as "sir" or "miss." Such formulations were built into the interaction, producing a structured, almost predictable response from both human beings. The artificiality of this half-rote activity hindered any real interaction, and the communicators operated at a level of unreality.

Although the legal sanctions for such unnatural relationships are nearly eliminated, the resultant psychological barriers to authentic transracial communication have been numerous, and despite the recent thrusts for black awareness and the dissolution of archaic racist laws, many whites and blacks *expect* to enter mock conversations. The remembrances of the past, for many persons, are too deeply imbedded to be uprooted with changes in rhetoric or law. Of course, these superficial interactions will continue to be, as they were previously, unproductive and, perhaps, pseudo-satisfying for many white persons. Those blacks, on the other hand, who engage in verbal interaction within the customary shell of black servility and white mastery will continue to find this ossified structure damaging to genuine communication. In fact, these lessons are easily learned by all persons who interact. To allow customary subservience or power a place in human interaction is to introduce an inevitable obstruction. This leads us to a discussion of the power variable as it relates to the race of the communicators.

Apart from, and yet alongside, the concept of customary subservience and mastery has been the notion of white racial superiority. In effect, whites often assumed attitudes of superiority or paternalism that caused them to be more expansive than their counterparts. Feeling themselves to be more powerful, they acted as if they were, even if the only reason for the assumption was a white skin. The less expansive counterpart, on the other hand, often felt himself to be less powerful.

The critical moments in interracial communication often come when blacks or other minorities assume different power roles from those expected of them. This, in effect, was the symbolism of the 1968 Black Power salute by Tommy Smith and John Carlos on the winners' stand at the Mexico City Olympics. Their assumption of a different style, unexpectedly, was one indication that blacks could not be depended upon to behave in traditional ways. Classroom examples of similar behavior patterns abound and have brought a new dimension to education. Recently in a university class, the black and chicano students dominated discussion and debate on theoretical and practical issues related to the course. In a way, their actions were demonstrative to the white students and teachers: The minorities had reversed the usual roles. The expansiveness of these minority students was one more manifestation that the control and manipulation of social behavior could be used by either group. However, such a situation is not in the best interest of open communication channels. It is merely a lesson in role changes, much like one practiced among black students in the late 1960's of having whites take seats in the rear of the room, in a reserved section, when noted black speakers were giving talks. As an object lesson, these practices were instructive, inasmuch as they showed whites what it was like to be discriminated against. But a continuation of this practice would only endanger the kind of interaction necessary for better communication.

We know, on the basis of evidence presented in an experiment on the power variable in communication experiments, that there exists a strong tendency in the direction of a relative preference for more powerful persons in one's group, and that this tendency is stronger when the subjects themselves are in a more powerful position.[11] Thus we can assume that in transracial situations, the way to increase effective interaction between persons is to encourage the exercise of power by all parties. In other words, a chicano is more likely to have a positive reaction to himself in a power position vis-à-vis the Anglo. But this has to work in both ways in the communicative experience to be meaningful. An Anglo without power and without the ability to exercise power only changes roles with the minority person who historically has been powerless.

## Trust and Suspicion in Transracial Communication

In another section, we have discussed willingness to communicate as a prerequisite for any effective human interaction. Willingness, however, does not cover the concept of assured anticipation that we recognize in the word *trust*. Therefore, this section is devoted to the place of trust in transracial interactions.

[11]Mauk Mulder, "The Power Variable in Communications," *Human Relations*, 13 (1960), 241–56.

If we begin with our understanding of anticipation in communication, we will be able to grasp the concept of trust as a *binding* element in relations between people. The order given to our human interactions by the unconscious mental aids that we get or create, such as stereotyping and anticipatory responses, makes our life easier. Because we know what to expect of our enemies or our friends, we live rather orderly lives, until our expectations are shown to be incorrect. If I am convinced that Junior Parker is my enemy and I expect him to put all kinds of obstacles in the way of a certain project that I have devised, and if then he acts in a manner contrary to my anticipation, it could be slightly unsettling. In a sense, we all bet on our enemies and friends by carving out certain positions for them, and if they do not fill those positions, they will disappoint us. After several meetings or a longer acquaintance with a person, our ability to anticipate his actions or reactions is increased. Usually trust is developed after we have observed certain patterns of behavior over a period of time. Thus predictability is one aspect of trust, but it is not the only element in the concept. As Morton Deutsch has said, the most common usages of the term have the additional meaning that "when trust is not fulfilled, the trusting individual perceives that he will be worse off if he trusts and his trust is not fulfilled than if he does not trust." Deutsch calls this motivational relevance.[12]

How, then, must trust be looked at in transracial communication? Most individuals are reluctant to engage in interactional activities that have potentially more negative than positive consequences. Blacks, Mexican-Amer-

[12]Morton Deutsch, "Trust and Suspicion," *Journal of Conflict Resolution*, 2 (1958), 266.

icans, Appalachian whites, and others, apart from ethnic backgrounds, are suspicious of an activity if what is predicted is not preferred and leads to behavior geared to reducing the negative motivational consequences.[13] *Racial trust* exists when Person A and Person B have similar levels of predictability and motivational relevance as regards each other. Person A expects and is willing to bet on the fulfillment of his expectation that Person B will respond in a given way; additionally, Person A is willing to do what Person B expects him to do. In such a situation, each perceives the other as being aware of his intent and perspective.[14] For a black person or a chicano to trust most whites, there has to be some understanding of intent, perspective, and a perception of trust in the white respondent. This is obviously true as it relates to any ethnic group; communication can be meaningful only on this level, because it is so easy for people who bear suspicion or hostility toward each other to miss the basic assumptions upon which a message rests. If that occurs, then the communicators are talking at different levels.

Such a situation can greatly aggravate suspicion, which exists "when each person expects the other person to produce a malevolent event in regard to himself and, in turn, is ready to produce a malevolent event for the other based upon this expectation."[15] The black person who has seen a series of negative consequences to his expectations is more likely to possess suspicion than the one who has not. His suspicion is based upon a certain degree of predictability and perception of the white per-

[13] *Ibid.*
[14] *Ibid.*, p. 268.
[15] *Ibid.*

son's malevolent intent. A black family in a southern city rushed the father of the family to an emergency ward of a hospital, only to be refused admittance. The father, who became exceedingly ill, informed his family that he never wanted to be taken to the hospital again. Thus, an event that was perceived in a fundamental sense to be detrimental to the father's welfare caused anger and suspicion. What had happened, from the fact that the man was taken to the hospital, was that the family had exercised trusting behavior. In the future, the people involved in this event will have conflicting tendencies to engage in or avoid engaging in trusting behavior as it relates to hospitals.

## Credibility

Credibility is not always the same as trust. The fact that we may believe a person will do what he says he will do, or act toward us in a certain way does not necessarily imply our acceptance of his ideas. Credibility is derived when in our past dealings with him we have come to be able to predict with considerable accuracy what his actions would be. Blacks in the South, for instance, had come to predict with precise accuracy the pronouncements and actions of politicians in some districts. When a late Georgia senator said, "I'll be dead before I see whites working for Negroes in my district," he was stating a segregationist's position, and his credibility with blacks was extremely high. So credibility cannot be equated entirely with trust.

In interracial situations, especially where there is a history of tension and distrust, it is often difficult to establish credibility. In fact, members of such ethnic groups frequently have to overcome prejudiced opinions before they can communicate their message, unless, of course, the message is demonstrative. Obvious attempts to don the mantle of credibility can cause violent rejection from the receiving group. There is one principal "credibility blunder" in most interracial situations: the how-do-you-feel or what-do-you-think syndrome. It is manifest in several ways, and usually starts as a sincere endeavor to show oneself credible. The "credibility blunder" assumes that the other communicator is omniscient on matters relating to his own ethnic group. This means, in the mind of the communication initiator, that there should be nothing the ethnic person should not know about any other person from that ethnic group. He must be knowledgeable of all historical and current facts and events, and most important of all, the peculiar slice of ethnic material that the communication initiator possesses. Furthermore, the ethnic receiver is presumed to be interested in the special knowledge used by the initiator to demonstrate credibility.

The "credibility blunder" is applicable only to the ethnic group representative of the special information used as a wedge to open communication. A typical case is that of a person of an ethnic group different from native Americans approaching a native American and saying, "What do you think about the Indians sitting in at those museums in the western states?" or to a chicano, "You Mexican-Americans ought to be proud of Jim Plunkett"; to a black person ,"Willie Mays must be your favorite hero," or to a white person, "Jerry West must make you feel good, playing basketball like he does." Of course, these statements and questions appear to us now to be immature attempts to build credibility, but

125

they are among the greatest causes of suspicion in trans-racial communication. They need not be artificial and trite if the communicator remembers that credibility should grow out of interaction rather than contrivance.

When a person is perceived to have contrived a "credibility blunder," the likelihood of his success in conveying credibility is significantly reduced. Studies by Hovland, by Berelson, and by Gandet have shown that some conversations derive their efficacy from the fact that the receivers of messages do not assume critical and defensive mental sets that are typical of situations where they know someone is out to influence them.[16] The person who enters an interracial communication by employing a "credibility blunder" sets the stage against himself, for he is perceived to be insincere.[17] Most people like to think that they reject obvious attempts at persuasion or establishment of personal credibility, and in interracial communication it is important that the exploitation of materials with ethnic content not serve to further the tension existing between people of different races. Inasmuch as the perception of artificiality in communication can hinder effective interracial interaction, a chief task of the would-be communicator is the avoidance of overt appeals to ethnicity that have no other purpose than the establishment of a link with the recipient of the message.

## Routinization of Communication

Transracial communication frequently falls victim to ritualization. Communicators go through carefully charted

[16]See Carl I. Hovland, Irving Janis, and Harold Kelley, *Communication and Persuasion: Psychological Studies of Opinion Change* (New Haven: Yale University Press, 1953), p. 22.

[17]Jack Daniel, "The Facilitation of White–Black Communication," *Journal of Communication*, 20 (1970), 134–41.

steps in order to give an impression of interest and involvement. Knowledge of the procedures is often gathered from observing others in similar situations and from an attempt to demonstrate personal involvement. Here it is necessary to indicate that the conscientious communicator usually falls into a formalized ritual without recognizing it. Formalization and ritualization become unacceptable when they displace real feelings and concerns. After all, the first person who responded in a certain fashion was probably not doing it as a ritual. However, ritual has an added dimension as we are using it in this section. It also carries with it the idea of a routine. Specifically, it refers to any formalized steps in interpersonal communication between persons of different races adhered to by habit. Such interaction engaged in unconsciously or without premeditation is ritualized. Let us take a look at a typical routinization chart. Figure 2 represents a finite number of possibilities for routinization, but it is possible to show every communication situation on such a chart.

Let us draw some implications from this chart. First, in this specialized example, when persons of different races interact at the level of a public greeting with a minimum degree of familiarity, the potential for routinization

## Routinization Chart

*FIGURE 2*

| Kind of Event | Degree of Familiarity | Potential for Routinization | Duration of Routine |
|---|---|---|---|
| Public greeting | minimum | high | long |
| Club meeting | maximum | low | initial |
| Party | minimum | high | short |

is high and is usually established for the length of inter-action. This is partly due to the associative ritualization of the public greeting; that is, a certain amount of ritual usually accompanies public greetings. So apart from trans-racial interaction, the potential for routinization is high. Such routinization is almost always set up as soon as the communicators make their interchange and lasts until the event is over. In fact, when a communicator attempts to alter the ritual, he might receive some annoying stares. The next time someone says to you, "How are you?" tell him exactly how you are and you will possibly wreck his day, because such a greeting is an accepted routine in our society. Only foreigners expect a thorough answer to this formalized question. For this reason, the public greeting has a high possibility for routinization. In this case, it does not matter whether the formalization is maximum or minimum, except in those instances where romance or business is involved. Then we have to say that the pos-sibility for routinization is low; the duration of routiniza-tion, if applicable, is short. While the formalization of the public greeting may be avoided, the communicators may engage in a routine associated with informal con-versation.

Secondly, the club-meeting example shows a maxi-mum degree of familiarity, a low potential for routiniza-tion, and an initial routinization. As a kind of interactive event, the club meeting is representative of sororities, fraternities, religious fellowships, and other associations where people unite with common beliefs and goals. In this example, there is a high degree of familiarity, and the potential for routinization is low because when peo-ple of different races know each other, there is enough common ground for them to share meaning without substituting routinization. Also, if routinization occurred in this instance, it would be initial. There seems to be movement toward a lessening of routinization when persons know each other in transracial communication. In cases where there is only minimum knowledge of each other, the routine is more likely to last the duration of the conversation. However, that is not necessarily the case. Some persons have been quick to point out to others instances when they felt conversations were rituals. In fact, many times when an ethnic-minority person says of a white that "he is patronizing," he means that his conversations are routines.

Third, in a party setting, we might have a minimum degree of familiarity, high potential for routinization, and a short duration of the routine. What this means is that it is highly likely that with people of different races, the less they know of each other, the greater the possibility for routinization; and that the routine will last some time beyond the initial interchange but not the full length of the conversation. The party setting is noted for informal conversations and small talk. Of course, it is possible for partygoers to have maximum familiarity with each other, but for this specialized chart, only the minimum degree of familiarity is suggested.

## CONVERSATIONS IN THE ROUTINE

### Public Greeting

This interactive event, as presented here, is characterized by a minimum degree of familiarity, a high potential for routinization, and a "long" duration of routine.

Thus, "How are you?" is usually answered in our society with "Fine," or some similar expression. Even "Not so well" or "Not so fine" is admissible, as long as the respondent does not take time to explain why his condition is so-and-so. Some people have been known to have the length of their smile timed precisely, so they can predict when to "turn it off."

### Item 1

| | |
|---|---|
| *Ethnic Person X:* | How are you? |
| *Ethnic Person Y:* | Fine. |

### Item II

| | |
|---|---|
| *Ethnic Person X:* | Hello, did you see Flip Wilson last night? |
| *Ethnic Person Y:* | No. |
| *Ethnic Person X:* | He sure was funny. |
| *Ethnic Person Y:* | I bet he was. |

### Item III

| | |
|---|---|
| *Ethnic Person X:* | Good morning. |
| *Ethnic Person Y:* | Good morning. |

In Item I, we have the basic routine between Americans regardless of race. Item II provides us with an insight into the routinized racial comment. While such a line may be given with sincerity, it is perceived as insincerity because the communicator attempts to move from a routinized greeting to what he thinks is more effective ground. However, what he sees as common ground is not novel to Person Y, because such tactics of identification are often used. Thus, the response of Y is negative. And it frequently happens that Y responds in the negative even if he is knowledgeable of the information requested in the question, because it is perceived as an opportunity to be as artificial and superficial as Person X. Therefore, in Item II, Person Y concludes in reaction to the statement that Flip Wilson was funny, "I'll bet he was."

## Club Meeting

The club meeting described in the routinization chart has a maximum degree of familiarity, low potential for routinization, and an initial duration. We assume, for this example, that a member of a club, fraternity, or sorority would have some familiarity with other members. In such cases, the potential for transracial routinization is low, and whatever routine does appear is only initial.

**Item I**

*Ethnic Person X:* The pyramids of Mexico are one indication of our cultural heritage.

*Ethnic Person Y:* We people of African descent brought that talent to Mexico. Look at the Egyptian pyramids.

This conversation, and others in this genre, are light games of ethnic competition usually engaged in when there is some familiarity with the other person.

**Item II**

*Ethnic Person X:* Looking at you, I wonder why the Japanese lost the last war.

*Ethnic Person Y:* Because we had better planes.

**Item III**

*Ethnic Person X:* Do you like Italian spaghetti?

*Ethnic Person Y:* Spaghetti came from China, man.

Each example above is demonstrative of the quick, light-hearted repartee among persons who know each other. Human communication is made easier in this situation, because the low potential for routinization allows people to explore their real selves.

## Party

### Item I

Ethnic Person X: Are you with John's company?
Ethnic Person Y: No, I'm just a friend.
Ethnic Person X: I have a colored friend you might know, Sam Williams?
Ethnic Person Y: Can't say I know him.
Ethnic Person X: Well, he used to work at the train station, and I would see him when I went down there.

### Item II

Ethnic Person X: What kind of work you do?
Ethnic Person Y: I'm an electrical engineer with Masons and Masons.
Ethnic Person X: That's mighty fine. You Japanese sure know how to get ahead. And they say you lost the war.
Ethnic Person Y: I'm an American, I fought in the war.
Ethnic Person X: Think I'll have another drink.

### Item III

Ethnic Person X: Hey, you Mexican?
Ethnic Person Y: I like to be called chicano.
Ethnic Person X: Don't you think that Chavez is causing lots of bad feelings among the races?
Ethnic Person Y: Nothing that wasn't already there.

In Item I, we have an example that makes use of a commonly employed prop to get into more serious conversation with someone who is unknown to you. Person X raises the initial question to ascertain information regarding status and friendship with the host. The reply by Person Y avoids the question of status and replies to the question by indicating his relationship to the host. Thus, the question of profession or vocation is left unanswered. However, Person X seizes the relationship between Person Y and the host as a way into the interracial circle. He states that he has a "colored friend" and, perhaps without knowing, gives Person Y a clue to his social awareness. Looking at Item II, we also see Person X indicating the extent of his social awareness. Thinking that he had given Person Y a compliment, he fails to recognize the narrowness of his perspective. In Item III, Person X not only lacks social awareness, but imputes the cause of ill will to Cesar Chavez. Variations of these routines can be found on most party circuits.

The ritual of interpersonal communication, with the illusions of contact and the ephemeral conversations, is aggravated when people interact transracially or transethnically. Awareness of the styles of routinization between persons of different races will prepare us for conversations that do not insult. Human beings possess interests and values that are not necessarily race-related, and the person who "grooves" with the context will not be embarrassed nor embarrassing.

## CONSENSUS: THE PLAGUE OF NORMALIZATION

Although consensus usually refers to agreement between persons regarding an issue or position, this is not the case in a transracial context. Here, consensus can be defined as group solidarity—for example, the pressure that whites might use to force minority members to accept their positions. Or it might be the end product of such solidarity—as of a militant group of native Americans marching with tomahawks into a college president's office. Whatever the case, consensus has assumed a new role in transracial contexts.

Normalization of communication cannot occur under acceptance of consensus by pressure. Frequently when whites and minority persons talk, there seem to be certain acceptances of objectives and norms when in fact there are not. Burk points out that "blacks used to be a good example of consensus. . . . From the outside there seemed to be agreement as to the second-class citizen role for blacks in the 'white man's world.' Many whites have since been rocked by the reality shock that has accompanied the realization that blacks may have always wanted something more." He continues, "The actual consensus in the case of black–white interaction was acceptance of the fact that there was no appropriate behavior pattern for blacks, save the black man's subordinate role to the white man. Compliance in the case of blacks was rationalized as the 'greatest good' because it benefited more people—whites."

Compliance by blacks in the situation described above is no indication of agreement. Possibly, persons engaged in transracial interactions may mistake tacit acceptance as agreement when it may indicate only a willingness to avoid problems. Unfortunately, this situation seldom minimizes problems; more often, it creates them. Lack of candor in any communication situation leads to mistrust and misunderstanding. In an interracial context, honesty is not just the best policy, it is an essential policy.

Initiating communication with people of other races

or ethnic groups, at times difficult, is easier than sustaining it. Because we tend to translate signs of the other's behavior into our own signal system, we are likely to experience what can be called "signal discontinuity" when a sign does not mean what we think it should. Signal discontinuity can occur as a result of conflicting behavior patterns emerging in a communication situation. Thus, what may seem to be consensus may only be a signal miscue. There is the story of two schoolteachers, one black and the other white, engaged in teacher chitchat about the horrors of the school system and some of their students. The white teacher, in recounting her experiences with one of her students, Dawn Davis, noticed the black teacher nodding her head. The white teacher asked, "Oh, do you know Dawn?" "No," replied the black teacher. The white teacher went on with her story but found it strange that the teacher would shake her head as if she knew the person when she did not. What she did not know was that many blacks nod their heads, not in agreement or consensus or knowledge, but as an indication of awareness of the speaker's ideas.

Therefore, our interaction with others can be greatly facilitated by an appreciation of the others' behaviors as reflected in communication signals. Normalization can occur despite the pressure for consensus when the communicators' perceptions of each other are realistic.

# Bibliography

ALLPORT, FLOYD H., *Theories of Perception and the Concept of Structure.* New York: John Wiley & Sons, Inc., 1955.

ALLPORT, GORDON W., *The Nature of Prejudice.* Reading, Mass.: Addison-Wesley Publishing Co., Inc., 1954.

ANDERSON, WALLACE L., and NORMAN C. STAGEBERG, eds., *Introductory Readings on Language.* New York: Holt, Rinehart & Winston, Inc., 1962.

ARGYLE, M., *The Psychology of Interpersonal Behavior.* Baltimore: Penguin Books, Inc., 1967.

ARONSON, ELLIOT, and D. LINDER, "Gain and Loss of Esteem as Determinants of Interpersonal Attractiveness," *Journal of Experimental Social Psychology,* 1 (1965), 156–71.

ARONSON, ELLIOT, and J. MILLS, "The Effect of Severity of Initiation on Liking for a Group," *Journal of Abnormal and Social Psychology,* 67 (1959), 31–36.

ARONSON, ELLIOT, and P. WORCHEL, "Similarity vs. Liking as Determinants of Interpersonal Attractiveness," *Psychonomic Science,* 5 (1966), 157–58.

BACKMAN, CARL W., and PAUL F. SECORD, "The Effect of Perceived Liking on Interpersonal Attraction," *Human Relations,* 12 (1959), 379–84.

BAKER, VIRGIL L., and RALPH GUBANKS, *Speech in Personal and Public Affairs.* New York: David McKay Co., Inc., 1965.

BAKONYR, STEFANO, "Divergence and Convergence in Culture and Communication," *Journal of Communication,* 8 (1958), 24–30.

BANDURA, ALBERT, and R. H. WALTERS, *Social Learning and Personality Development*. New York: Holt, Rinehart & Winston, Inc., 1963.

BARKER, LARRY, and ROBERT KIBLER, Eds. *Speech Communication Behavior*. Englewood Cliffs, N.J.: Prentice-Hall, Inc., 1971.

BARNLUND, DEAN C., ed. *Interpersonal Communication: Survey and Studies*. Boston: Houghton Mifflin Company, 1968.

BARON, PAUL, *Communications, Computers and People*. Santa Monica, Calif.: Rand Corporation, 1965.

BARRY, SIR GERALD, *Communication and Language: Networks of Thought and Action*. London: MacDonald, 1965.

BEARDSLEE, DAVID C., and MICHAEL WERTHEIMER, *Readings in Perception*. New York: Van Nostrand Reinhold Company, 1958.

BENNIS, WARREN G., KENNETH D. BENNE, and ROBERT CHIN, eds. *The Planning of Change: Readings in the Behavioral Sciences*. New York: Holt, Rinehart & Winston, Inc., 1962.

BERELSON, BERNARD, *Content Analysis in Communication Research*. New York: The Free Press, 1952.

BERELSON, BERNARD, and GARY A. STEINER, *Human Behavior: An Inventory of Scientific Findings*. New York: Harcourt Brace Jovanovich, Inc., 1964.

BERGER, E. M., "The Relation Between Expressed Acceptance of Self and Expressed Acceptance of Others," *Journal of Abnormal and Social Psychology*, 47 (1952), 778–82.

BERLO, DAVID K., *The Process of Communication*. New York: Holt, Rinehart & Winston, Inc., 1960.

BETTELHEIM, B., and M. JANOWITZ, *Dynamics of Prejudice*. New York: Harper & Row, Publishers, 1950.

BION, W. R., *Experiences in Groups*. New York: Basic Books, Inc., Publishers, 1961.

BIRDWHISTILL, RAY L., *Introduction to Kinesics: An Annotation System For Analysis of Body Motion and Gesture*. Washington, D.C.: Foreign Service Institute, Department of State, 1952.

BLAKE, ROBERT R., and GLENN V. RAMSEY, ed., *Perception: An Approach to Personality*. New York: The Ronald Press Company, 1951.

BOGARDUS, E. S., "Measuring Social Distance," *Journal of Applied Sociology*, 9 (1925), 299–308.

BORDEN, GEORGE A., RICHARD B. GREGG, and THEODORE G. GROVE, *Speech Behavior and Human Interaction*. Englewood Cliffs, N.J.: Prentice-Hall, Inc., 1969.

BOSMAJIAN, HAIG A., ed., *The Rhetoric of Nonverbal Communication*. Glenview, Ill.: Scott, Foresman and Company, 1971.

BRAM, JOSEPH, *Language and Society*. New York: Random House, Inc., 1955.

BRAMEL, D., "Interpersonal Attraction, Hostility and Perception," in *Experimental Social Psychology*, ed. Judson Mills. New York: The Macmillan Company, 1969.

BROWN, ROGER, *Words and Things*. The Free Press, 1958.

BROXTON, J. A., "A Test of Interpersonal Attraction Predictions Derived from Balance Theory," *Journal of Abnormal and Social Psychology*, 63 (1963), 394–97.

BRUNER, JEROME S., JACQUELINE J. GOODNOW, and GEORGE A. AUSTIN, *A Study of Thinking*. New York: John Wiley & Sons, 1956.

BURKE, REDMOND AMBROSE, *Culture and Communication Through the Ages*. Chicago: De Paul University Library, 1953.

BURNSTEIN, E., and P. WORCHEL, "Arbitrariness of Frustration and Its Consequences for Aggression in a Special Situation," *Journal of Personality*, 30 (1962), 528–40.

BYRNE, DONN E., "Interpersonal Attraction and Attitude Similarity," *Journal of Abnormal and Social Psychology*, 62 (1961), 713–15.

BYRNE, DONN E., and G. L. CLORE, JR., "Predicting Interpersonal Attraction Toward Strangers Presented in Three Different Stimulus Modes," *Psychonomic Science*, 4 (1966), 239–40.

BYRNE, DONN E., and T. J. WONG, "Racial Prejudice, Interpersonal Attraction and Assumed Dissimilarity of Attitudes," *Journal of Abnormal and Social Psychology*, 65 (1962), 246–52.

CAMPBELL, JAMES H., and HAL W. HELPER, eds., *Dimensions in Communication*. Belmont, Calif.: Wadsworth Publishing Co., Inc., 1956.

CARPENTER, EDMUND SNOW, and MARSHALL McLUHAN, eds., *Explorations in Communications*. Boston: Beacon Press, 1960.

CARTWRIGHT, DARWIN, and ALVIN ZANDER, eds., *Group Dynamics: Research and Theory* (2nd ed.). Evanston, Ill.: Row, Peterson & Co., 1960.

CAUTER, T., and J. S. DOWNHAM, *The Communication of Ideas: A Study of Contemporary Influences upon Urban Life*. London: Chatto & Windus, 1954.

CHASE, STUART, *The Tyranny of Words*. New York: Harcourt Brace Jovanovich, Inc., 1938.

CHERRY, COLIN, *On Human Communication*. New York: Science Editions, 1961.

CHURCH, JOSEPH, *Language and the Discovery of Reality: A Developmental Psychology of Cognition*. New York: Vintage Books, Random House, Inc., 1961.

COHEN, ARTHUR, *Attitude Change and Social Influences*. New York: Basic Books, Inc., Publishers, 1964.

COWEN, D., J. LANDES, and D. E. SCHAET, "The Effects of Mild Frustration on the Expression of Prejudiced Attitudes," *Journal of Abnormal and Social Psychology*, 58 (1959), 33–38.

DANCE, FRANK E. X., "A Helical Model of Communication," in *Foundations of Communication Theory*, eds. Kenneth K. Sereno and C. David Mortensen. New York: Harper & Row, Publishers, 1970.

DANCE, FRANK E. X., ed., *Human Communication Theory*. New York: Holt, Rinehart & Winston, Inc., 1967.

DANIEL, JACK L., "The Facilitation of White–Black Communication," *Journal of Communication*, 20 (1970), 134–41.

DANIELS, ROGER, *The Politics of Prejudice.* New York: Atheneum Publishers, 1968.

DARLEY, J. M., and E. BERSCHEID, "Increased Liking as a Result of the Anticipation of Personal Contact," *Human Relations,* 20 (1967), 29–40.

DAVIDSON, J., "Cognitive Familiarity and Dissonance Reduction," in *Conflict, Decision, and Dissonance,* ed. Leon Festinger. Stanford, Calif.: Stanford Press, 1964.

DAVIS, K. E., and E. E. JONES, "Changes in "Interpersonal Perception as a Means of Reducing Cognitive Dissonance," *Journal of Abnormal and Social Psychology,* 61 (1960), 402–10.

DEUTSCH, M., and M. E. COLLINS, "The Effect of Public Policy in Housing Projects upon Interracial Attitudes," in *Readings in Social Psychology* (3rd ed.), eds. Eleanor Maccoby, T. M. Newcomb, and E. L. Hartley. New York: Holt, Rinehart & Winston, Inc., 1958.

DEUTSCH, M., and L. SOLOMON, "Reactions to Evaluations by Others as Influenced by Self-evaluation," *Sociometry,* 22 (1959), 93–112.

DICKOFF, H., "Reactions to Evaluations by Another Person as a Function of Self-evaluation and the Interaction Context." Unpublished doctoral dissertation, Duke University, 1961. Also reported in Jones, E. E., *Ingratiation,* q.v.

DITTES, J. E., "Attractiveness of Group as Function of Self-esteem and Acceptance by Group," *Journal of Abnormal and Social Psychology,* 59 (1959), 77–82.

DORWART, W., R. EZERMAN, M. LEWIS, and D. ROSENHAN, The Effect of Brief Social Deprivation on Social and Nonsocial Reinforcement," *Journal of Personality and Social Psychology,* 2 (1965), 111–15.

DUNCAN, HUGH D., *Communication and Social Order.* Totowa, N.J.: The Bedminster Press, Inc., 1962.

————, *Symbols in Society.* New York: Oxford University Press, Inc., 1968.

EDWARDS, A. L., "Political Frames of Reference as a Factor Influencing Recognition," *Journal of Abnormal and Social Psychology,* 36 (1941), 34–50.

FELDMAN, SHEL, ed., *Cognitive Consistency*. New York: Academic Press, Inc., 1966.

FESTINGER, LEON, "Group Attraction and Membership," in *Group Dynamics: Research and Theory*, eds. D. Cartwright and A. Zander. Evanston, Ill.: Row, Peterson & Co., 1953.

————, *A Theory of Cognitive Dissonance*. Evanston, Ill.: Row, Peterson & Co., 1957.

————, "A Theory of Social Comparison Processes," *Human Relations*, 7 (1954), 117–40.

FESTINGER, L., A. PEPITONE, and T. M. NEWCOMB, "Some Consequences of Deindividuation in a Group," *Journal of Abnormal and Social Psychology*, 47 (1952), 382–89.

FESTINGER, LEON, STANLEY SCHACHTER, and KURT W. BACK, *Social Pressures in Informal Groups: A Study of Human Factors in Housing*. New York: Harper & Row, Publishers, 1950.

FINE, BERNARD J., "Conclusion-Drawing Communicator Credibility and Anxiety as Factors in Opinion Change," *Journal of Abnormal and Social Psychology*, 54 (1957), 369–74.

GEWIRTZ, JACOB L., and DONALD M. BAER, "Deprivation and Satiation of Social Reinforcers as Drive Conditions," *Journal of Abnormal and Social Psychology*, 57 (1958), 165–72.

————, "The Effect of Brief Social Deprivation on Behaviors for a Social Reinforcer," *Journal of Abnormal and Social Psychology*, 56 (1958), 49–56.

GLENN, EDMUND S., "Meaning and Behavior in Communication and Culture," *Journal of Communication*, 16 (1966), 248–72.

GOLDBERG, GORDON N., CHARLES A. KIESLER, and BARRY E. COLLINS, "Interpersonal Attraction and Situational Definition as Determinants of the Spacing of Interacting Individuals," *Sociometry*, 32 (1969), 43–53.

GREENBERG, JOSEPH H., ed., *Universals of Language*. Cambridge, Mass.: The M.I.T. Press, 1963.

GRIFFIN, KIM, and BOBBY R. PATTON, eds., *Basic Readings in Interpersonal Communication.* New York: Harper & Row, Publishers, 1971.

GULLAHORN, JOHN T., "Distance and Friendship as Factors in the Gross Interaction Matrix," *Sociometry,* 15 (1952), 123–34.

GUMPERZ, JOHN J., and DELL HYMES, *The Ethnography of Communication.* Washington, D.C.: American Anthropological Association, 1964.

HACKETT, HERBERT, *Understanding and Being Understood.* New York: Longmans, Green, 1967.

HALL, EDWARD T., *The Silent Language.* New York: Doubleday & Company, Inc., 1959; Fawcett Books, 1961.

HALL, ROBERT A., JR., *Leave Your Language Alone!* Ithaca, N.Y.: Linguistics, 1950.

HAMBLIN, R., "Group Integration During a Crisis," *Human Relations,* 11 (1958), 67–76.

HANEY, WILLIAM U., *Communication: Patterns and Incidents.* Homewood, Ill.: Richard D. Irwin, Inc., 1960.

HARE, A. PAUL, EDGAR F. BARGATTA, and ROBERT F. BALES, eds., *Small Groups: Studies in Social Interaction.* New York: Alfred A. Knopf, Inc., 1955.

HARVEY, O. J., "Personality Factors in Resolution of Conceptual Incongruities," *Sociometry,* 25 (1962), 336–52.

HARVEY, O. J., H. H. KELLEY, and M. M. SHAPIRO, "Reactions to Unfavorable Evaluations of the Self Made by Other Persons," *Journal of Personality,* 25 (1957), 393–411.

HARVEY, O. J., and JEANNE RUTHERFORD, "Gradual and Absolute Approaches to Attitude Change," *Sociometry,* 21 (1958), 61–68.

HAYAKAWA, S. I., *Language in Thought and Action.* New York: Harcourt Brace Jovanovich, Inc., 1964.

HEBB, D. O., *Organization of Behavior.* New York: John Wiley & Sons, Inc., 1949.

HEIDER, FRITZ, *The Psychology of Interpersonal Relations.* New York: John Wiley & Sons, Inc., 1958.

**143**

HELLER, LOUIS G., and JAMES MACRES, "Toward a General Linguistic and Nonlinguistic Sociocultural Typology and Its Dynamics," *Journal of Communication*, 19 (1969), 285–300.

HOFFMAN, L. R., "Similarity of Personality: A Basis for Interpersonal Attraction?" *Sociometry*, 21 (1958), 300–308.

HOGGART, RICHARD, *The Uses of Literacy*. Boston: Beacon Press, 1961.

HOLTZMAN, PAUL D., *The Psychology of Speaker's Audiences*. Glenview, Ill.: Scott, Foresman and Company, 1970.

HOMANS, G. C., *Social Behavior: Its Elementary Forms*. New York: Harcourt Brace Jovanovich, Inc., 1961.

HOVLAND, CARL I., et al., *The Order of Presentation in Persuasion*. New Haven: Yale University Press, 1959.

HOVLAND, CARL I., and IRVING JANIS, *Personality and Persuasibility*. New Haven: Yale University Press, 1959.

HOVLAND, CARL I., IRVING L. JANIS, and HAROLD H. KELLEY, *Communication and Persuasion; Psychological Studies of Opinion Change*. New Haven: Yale University Press, 1953.

HOVLAND, CARL I., and H. A. PRITZKER, "Extent of Opinion Change as Function of Amount of Change Advocated," *Journal of Abnormal and Social Psychology*, 54 (1957), 257–61.

JAMES, A., and A. J. LOTT, "Reward Frequency and the Formation of Positive Attitudes Toward Group Members," *Journal of Social Psychology*, 62 (1964), 111–15.

JANIS, I. L., and S. TESHBACK, "Effects of Fear-Arousing Communications," *Journal of Abnormal and Social Psychology*, 48 (1953), 78–92.

JOHNSON, WENDELL, *People in Quandaries: The Semantics of Personal Adjustment*. New York: Harper & Row, Publishers, 1946.

JONES, E. E., *Ingratiation: A Social Psychological Analysis*. New York: Appleton-Century-Crofts, 1964.

JONES, E. E., K. J. GERGEN, and K. E DAVIS, "Some Determinants of Reactions to Being Approved or Disapproved as a Person," *Psychological Monographs*, 76, No. 521 (1962).

KATZ, E., and PAUL F. LAZARSFELD, *Personal Influence: The Part Played by People in the Flow of Mass Communication.* New York: The Free Press, 1955.

KLAPPER, JOSEPH T., *The Effects of Mass Communication.* New York: The Free Press, 1960.

LADO, ROBERT, *Linguistics Across Cultures.* Ann Arbor: University of Michigan Press, 1957.

LANGELLE, VERNON A., "Prejudice: Its Dynamics & Consequences," *Journal of Communication,* 6 (1956), 124–34.

LINDZEY, GARDNER, ed., *Assessment of Human Motives.* New York: Grove Press, Inc., 1960.

————, *Handbook of Social Psychology.* Reading, Mass.: Addison-Wesley Publishing Co., Inc., 1954.

LOTT, A. J., and B. E. LOTT, "Group Cohesiveness, Communication Level, and Conformity," *Journal of Abnormal and Social Psychology,* 62 (1961), 408–12.

McLUHAN, H. MARSHALL, *Culture Is Our Business.* New York: McGraw-Hill Book Company, 1970.

————, *The Medium Is the Message.* New York: Bantam Books, Inc., 1967.

————, *Understanding Media: The Extensions of Man.* New York: McGraw-Hill Book Company, 1965.

MASSERMAN, JULES HOMAN, *Communication and Community.* New York: Grune & Stratton, Inc., 1965.

MATSON, FLOYD W., and ASHLEY MONTAGUE, eds., *The Human Dialogue: Perspectives On Communication.* New York: The Free Press, 1967.

MEENES, H., "A Comparison of Racial Stereotypes of 1930 and 1942," *Journal of Social Psychology,* 17 (1943), 327–36.

MEERLOO, JOOST ABRAHAM MAURITS, *Unobtrusive Communication: Essays in Psycholinguistics.* Asser, The Netherlands: Van Gorcum, 1964.

MILLER, GEORGE A., *Language and Communication.* New York: McGraw-Hill Book Company, 1951.

————, *The Psychology of Communication.* New York: Basic Books, Inc., Publishers, 1967.

MOWRER, O. HOBART, *Learning Theory and the Symbolic Process.* New York: John Wiley & Sons, Inc., 1960.

NIDA, EUGENE A., *Linguistic Interludes.* Glendale, Calif.: Summer Institute of Linguistics, 1947.

NORTHRUP, S. C., and HELEN H. LIVINGSTON, eds., *Cross-Cultural Understanding, Epistemology in Anthropology.* New York: Harper & Row, Publishers, 1964.

OGAWA, DENNIS M., *From Japs to Japanese: Evolution of Japanese-American Stereotypes.* Unpublished book manuscript, University of Hawaii, 1970.

RICH, A. L., *An Experimental Study of the Nature of Communication to a Deviate in High and Low Cohesive Groups.* Unpublished dissertation, University of California at Los Angeles, 1968.

RIESMAN, DAVID, *The Lonely Crowd.* New Haven: Yale University Press, 1950.

ROKEACH, MILTON, *Beliefs, Attitudes and Values.* San Francisco: Jassey-Bass Inc., 1968.

ROSNOW, RALPH L., and EDWARD J. ROBINSON, eds., *Experiments in Persuasion.* New York: Academic Press, Inc., 1967.

RUESCH, JURGEN, and GREGORY BATESON, *Communication: The Social Matrix of Psychiatry.* New York: W. W. Norton & Company, Inc., 1951.

RUESCH, JURGEN, and WELDON KIES, *Nonverbal Communication: Notes on the Visual Perception of Human Relations.* Berkeley: University of California Press, 1956.

SAPORTA, SOL, ed., *Psycholinguistics: A Book of Readings.* New York: Holt, Rinehart & Winston, Inc., 1961.

SCHEAH, THOMAS A., ALFRED S. HAYES, and MARY CATHERINE BATESON, eds., *Approaches to Semiotics: Cultural Anthropology; Education; Linguistics; Psychiatry; Psychology.* The Hague, Netherlands: Mouton, 1964.

SCHRAMM, WILBUR LANG, *The Science of Human Communication: New Directions and Findings in Communication Research.* New York: Basic Books, Inc., Publishers, 1963.

SCHRAMM, WILBUR, ed., *The Process and Effects of Mass Communication*. Urbana: University of Illinois Press, 1954.

SEAGO, D. W., "Stereotypes Before Pearl Harbor and After," *Journal of Psychology*, 23 (1947), 53–63.

SERENO, KENNETH K., and C. DAVID MORTENSEN, eds., *Foundations of Communication Theory*. New York: Harper & Row, Publishers, 1970.

SHANNON, CLAUDE E., and WARREN WEAVER, *The Mathematical Theory of Communications*. Urbana: University of Illinois Press, 1962.

SHERIF, MUZAFER, O. J. HARVEY, B. J. WHITE, W. R. HOOD, and CAROLYN W. SHERIF, *Experimental Study of Positive and Negative Intergroup Attitudes Between Experimentally Produced Groups: Robbers' Cave Study*. Norman: University of Oklahoma, 1954 (multilithed).

SHERIF, MUZAFER, and CARL I. HOVLAND, *Social Judgment; Assimilation and Contrast Effects in Communication and Attitude Change*. New Haven: Yale University Press, 1961.

SHERIF, MUZAFER, and CAROLYN W. SHERIF, eds., *Attitude, Ego Involvement and Change*. New York: John Wiley & Sons, Inc., 1967.

SIGALL, H., and ELLIOT ARONSON, "Opinion Change and the Gain–Loss Model of Interpersonal Attraction," *Journal of Experimental Social Psychology*, 3 (1967), 178–88.

SIMPSON, GEORGE, and JOHN M. YINGER, *Racial and Cultural Minorities*. New York: Harper and Row, Publishers, 1965.

SMITH, ALFRED G., ed., *Communication and Culture: Readings in the Codes of Human Interaction*. New York: Holt, Rinehart & Winston, Inc., 1966.

SMITH, ARTHUR L., *Toward Transracial Communication*, Center Monograph Series, No. 1. Los Angeles: UCLA Afro-American Studies Center, 1970.

SMITH, BRUCE LANNES, HAROLD D. LASSWELL, and RALPH D. CASEY, *Propaganda, Communication and Public Opinion*. Princeton, N.J.: Princeton University Press, 1946.

STEWART, DANIEL K., *The Psychology of Communication.* New York: Funk & Wagnalls, 1969.

STEWART, EDWARD I., "The Simulation of Cultural Differences," *Journal of Communication*, 16 (1966), 291–304.

STOCK, D., "An Investigation into the Intercorrelations Between the Self-concept and Feelings Directed Toward Other Persons and Groups," *Journal of Consulting Psychology*, 13 (1949), 176–80.

TAGIURI, RENATO, and LUIGI PETRULLO, eds., *Person Perception and Interpersonal Behavior.* Palo Alto, Calif.: Stanford University Press, 1958.

WASHBURN, DONALD E., "Intrapersonal Communication in a Jungian Perspective," *Journal of Communication*, 14 (1964), 131–35.

WATHEN-DUNN, WEIANT, ed., *Models for the Perception of Speech and Visual Form.* Cambridge, Mass.: The M.I.T. Press, 1967.

WATZEAWICK, PAUL, *An Anthology of Human Communication.* Palo Alto, Calif.: Science & Behavior Books, Inc., 1964.

WATZEAWICK, PAUL, JANET HELMICK BEAVIN, and DON D. JACKSON, *Pragmatics of Human Communication: A Study of Interactional Patterns, Pathologies and Paradoxes.* New York: W. W. Norton & Company, Inc., 1967.

WEISS, WALTER, and B. J. FINE, "Opinion Change as a Function of Some Intrapersonal Attitudes of Communicators," *Journal of Abnormal and Social Psychology*, 51 (1955), 246–53.

WHORF, BENJAMIN LEE, *Language, Thought and Reality.* Cambridge, Mass.: The M.I.T. Press, 1956.

WHYTE, WILLIAM H., JR., *Is Anybody Listening?* New York: Simon & Schuster, Inc., 1952.

WIENER, NORBERT, *The Human Use of Human Beings.* New York: Doubleday & Company, Inc., 1956.

ZANDER, A., and A. HAVELIN, "Social Comparison and Interpersonal Attraction," *Human Relations*, 13 (1960), 21–32.

**148**

# Index

Abasi, 26
Accessibility, 52, 53
  flexibility, 53
  proximity, 53
Affectation, 56
African Culture, 27
  languages, 37
  professional, 26
  religions, 26
Alabama, 75
"All in the Family," 96
American Indians, 30, 32
  pueblo, 32
Anglo-Saxon, 85, 89
Apache, 91
Appalachian Hillbillies, 88
Asafo, 34
Asian-Americans, 30
Attica, 112
Austin, J. L., 101
Authoritarian, 29
Availability, 44, 53
  mental, 44
  physical, 44

Banton, Michael, 112
Baraka, Imamu, 34
Barnlund, Dean C., 13, 14
Bascom, William, 26
BAV (beliefs, attitudes, values), 64
Benedict, Ruth, 29
Bennett, John, 29
Bentley, Arthur F., 78
Berlo, David K., 18
Bias, 78
Black Americans, 26, 32
Black English, 37, 38
  biddy, 37
  eagle, 39

Black English (cont.)
  Geechee, 37
  goober, 37
  Gullah, 37
  hawk, 39
  okra, 37
  plurals, 39
  samba, 37
  verbs, 38
  functions, 41
  styles, 36
    copping a plea, 41, 42
    gripping, 41, 42
    jiving, 41
    rapping, 41, 42
    running it down, 41, 42
    shucking, 41, 42
    signifying, 41, 42
    sounding, 41
Black idioms, 39, 40
  coming down hard, 40
  community language, 39
Black Slang, 40, 41
  Ain't it funky, now?, 41
  A.P.T., 41
  bitch, 41
  blade, 40
  bogarting, 41
  check it out, 41
  hype, 41
  mean, 41
  mellow, 41
  ride, 40
  set, 41
  split, 41
  wheels, 41
Bon Dieu, 26
Booty, 58
"Brother," 35
Bunker, Archie, 96

# Index

Cadillacs, 34
California, 20, 40, 88
Cash, W. J., 107
Castillo, Juan, 45
Caucasian, 20
Chavez, Cesar, 133
Chicago, 39
Chicanos, 30
Chryslers, 34
Church, Joseph, 27
Cobbs, Price, 36
Co-cultural, 26
Cognitive development, 76
Cognitive process, 59
Communication, 10
  cross-cultural, 30
  direct, 11
  dyads, 49, 50, 51
  explicit, 11
  gestural, 10
  implicit, 11
  inadequate perception, 11
  indirect, 11
  intergroup, 49
  interpersonal, 13, 14, 49, 50
  lack of skill, 75
  mass, 49
  pictorial, 11
  process, 10
  purpose, 14
  structurization, 49, 50
  symbol, 10
  transracial, 4, 9, 10–17, 20, 27, 36,
    39, 44, 49–59, 63–70, 77, 95,
    101–22
  verbal, 10
Communicator, 11, 12
  status, 18
Conceptualizations, 10
Confrontation, 12
Connectedness, 71
Consensus, 133–35
Constitution, 87
Contextual influence, 29
Crazy nigger, 16
Credibility, 124
"Credibility blunder," 125
Cultural background, 26
Cultural behavior, 25
Cultural context, 11
Cultural differences, 29
Cultural grouping, 25
Cultural reality, 25

Culture, 25
  incongruence, 28
  Oriental, 25
  Western, 25

Dallas, 39
Dance, 13
Daniel, Jack, 126
Davis, Sammy (Jr.), 118
Defense mechanisms, 52
Definitional context, 9
Democratic, 29
Deutsch, Morton, 122
Dewey, John, 78
Duncan, Hugh, 83

Educable mental retardates, 117
Efik, 37
Eisenstadt, Shmuel N., 29
Engagees, 66, 67
Ethnic, 44
  dissimilarities, 45
  perspective, 66, 68
  similarities, 45
Ethnic group, 9
Ethnic identity, 10
Ethnicity, 20
Ethnocentric, 88
Exline, Ralph, 105

Family, 35, 36
  blood, 36
  extended, 35
  member, 36
  mother, 36
  skin, 36
  society, 35
Fearing, Franklin, 12
Flesh-colored, 92
Furbay, Albert, 105

Georgia, 37
Giovanni, Nikki, 34
God of Africa, 26
Grace Episcopal Cathedral Church,
  90
Gray, David, 105
Grier, William H., 36

Hall, Edward, 30, 32
Hanu-Claus, 88
Helical model, 13
Hernandez, Carlos, 45
Hernton, Calvin, 106
Herskovits, Melville, 26
Heuristic, 14
Hovland, E., 126

Ibo, 37
Illocutionary acts, 101–2
Impressions, 19
Influential factors, 19
    distant, 19
    immediate, 19
Initiator, 11, 12, 64, 67
    primary, 11, 12
    secondary, 11, 12
Interaction, 12
    dynamic, 10, 11
    symbolic, 10, 11
Interactive event, 129
Interethnic, 9, 14
Intervening symbolism, 106
Intervention, 43, 45

Jackson, Jesse (Rev.), 43
Janheinz, Jahn, 27, 84
Janis, Irving, 126
Japanese, 29, 144
    Americans, 73
    norm, 30
Jesus Christ, 96
Jews, 29
    European, 29
    North African, 29

Karenga, Maulana, 96
Kelley, Harold, 126
Knower, Franklin, 105
Kochman, Thomas, 41
Krasner, Leonard, 51

Laissez-faire, 29
Language, 37
    grammar, 37
    vocabulary, 47
Lee, Don, 34
Lewin, Kurt, 29

Linguistic regularity, 57–59
Linkage, 11, 12
    faulty, 17
    recurring, 12
Lippitt, Ronald, 29
Locutionary acts, 101
Louisiana Cajuns, 88
Lundberg, George, 10

MacLean, Malcolm S., 78
Man, 27
Mande, 37
Mayflower, 39
Mays, Willie, 125
McKnight, Robert, 29
Media, 11
Messages, 12
    verbal, 12
Metacommunication, 103–5
Mexican-American, 21, 30
Miller, George A., 18
"Miss America," 94
"Miss Black America," 94
Models, 63
    circular, 63
    helical, 13, 63
    linear, 63
Monoethnicity, 92
Muhammad Ali, 84
Multiethnic, 30, 63, 92
    harmony, 30, 63

Nommo, 84
Normalization, 55, 57, 59
Nude look, 92

Ogawa, Dennis, 74
Olorun, 26
Operation Breadbasket, 43
Orientation, 27

Passin, Herbert, 29
Perception, 26
Perlocutionary acts, 101
Personality, 20
"Play the Dozens," 43
Plunkett, Jim, 125
Pontiac, Michigan, 73
Power, 118

# Index

Prejudging, 18
Public arena, 63
Puerto Rican, 73

Race, 17
  Place, 73
  Supremacy, 73
Racism, 86, 90, 91
Rio Grande, 32
Rockefeller, Nelson (Gov.), 112
Rokeach, Milton, 71
Routinization, 126–29

Saint Soul, 88
San Francisco, 90
Santa Claus, 88
Sapir, Edward, 10
Schuette, Dorothy, 105
Seattle, 39
Sensitivity, 54
Sex, 105–11
Sexism, 111
Shared meanings, 15, 16, 115
Shrine of the Black Madonna, 97
Sinatra, Frank, 118
"Sister," 35
"Sizing Up," 57
Smith, Alfred G., 28
Smith, Arthur L., 41
Smith, Lillian, 107
Social climates, 29
Social-symbol reproducibility, 57–59
Socialization, 83
Society, 64
  complex, 64
  diverse, 64
Source, 64
South Carolina, 37
Spartans, 91
Speaker, 64
Spirit of Detroit, 89
Split-level acquaintances, 79
Status, 73
"Status gap," 112
Stereotyping, 74
Stratification, 111, 112
  horizontal, 116
  thinking, 112
Structure, 51
Structurization, 12, 28
  complex, 12
  simple, 12

Structurization (cont.)
  spatial, 12
  temporal, 12
Subtle agenda, 104
Symbol(s), 83–87
  hegemony, 85
  imperialism, 85–86
  perception, 83
  pluralism, 87
  structuring, 83
Symbolic reverse, 117

Task appreciation, 54
Time, 30–34
  African People's, 31, 33
  buy, 31
  commercial, 31, 34
  differential, 32  42
  hang loose, 31, 33
  lose, 31
  make, 31
  saving, 31
  waste, 31
Toch, Hans, 78
Trust, 122
Turner, Lorenzo, 37
Twi, 37

Universal context, 65
UCLA Center for Afro-American
  Studies, 112

Vertical hierarchy, 111

Wale, Ojekan, 45
Wallace, George, 97
Washington, 73
West, Jerry, 125
White, Ralph K., 29
Willingness, 51
Winans, James, 43

Yiddish, 58
  chutzpah, 58
Yoruba, 37

Zapata, Emiliano, 118
Zulu, 91